And Life Begins

By David Lawson

With the greatest thanks to:
Hilary, J.D. & Kelly and the girls
Melissa & Roy, Mike & Susan, and my mom, Linda

To my friends and colleagues whose encouragement kept me going:
Greg & Tiffany, Brian, and Dan

To the great medical staff and team at:
Breese Memorial Hospital
St. Elizabeth's Hospital – O'Fallon
Dr. Mary Agne

Lastly:
To the unknown chaplain of St. Elizabeth's Hospital
and
To my Creator, who saw fit to give me another day

A 10% donation from the sale of the book will be forwarded to the St. Elizabeth's Foundation in O'Fallon, IL for the treatment and care of stroke survivors and for continued research into the prevention of strokes.

HSHS St. Elizabeth's Hospital
One St. Elizabeth's Boulevard
O'Fallon, IL 62269
618.234.2120
www.steliz.org

Further information on strokes can be found at the following sites:

The National Stroke Association
www.stroke.org

Center For Disease Control and Prevention
www.cdc.gov/stroke

The Mayo Clinic
www.mayoclinic.org/diseases-conditions/stroke/diagnosis-treatment/drc-20350119

Barnes Jewish Hospital Stroke Center
www.barnesjewish.org/Medical-Services/Neurology-Neurosurgery/Stroke-Center

Contents

Introduction

IN 2017, STATISTICS PROVIDED BY THE CENTER FOR DISEASE CONTROL AND PREVENTION (CDC), about 795,000 individuals each year experience a stroke in the United States. Of these cases, about 610,000 are first-time victims, with the remaining 185,000 occurring in people who previously experienced a stroke. On average, someone in the United States suffers a stroke every forty seconds, even worse, someone dies every four minutes as a result of a stroke.

Strokes know no age boundaries or limits. Historically considered an elderly affliction, strokes can occur at any age and severity. In 2009, hospitals reported that 34% of stroke patients were under the age of 65. Hypertension, heart disease, diabetes and excessive stress are the main contributors of strokes, making them the fifth leading cause of deaths in the United States, with about 140,000 or 1 out of 20 deaths are attributed to strokes.

The vast majority, about 87%, are classified as ischemic (the blockage of a blood vessel that supplies blood to the brain). The most common condition for the obstruction is the development of fatty deposits that line the vessel walls, a condition known as atherosclerosis. The deposits can cause two types of obstructions:

- Cerebral thrombosis – the development of a blood clot which develops in the narrowest or clogged point in the vessel.
- Cerebral embolism – a clot that is formed in another location in the body, usually the heart or other large arteries of the chest and neck. A portion of the clot dislodges, enters the bloodstream and travels to the brain's blood vessel. Once the clot reaches a point that is too narrow to let it pass, a blockage occurs. Another cause of embolism

is an irregular heartbeat or atrial fibrillation, which creates a condition where clots form in the heart, dislodge and travel to the brain.

Strokes are estimated to cost about $34 billion each year, which include the cost of healthcare services, medicine, rehabilitation, and missed time from employment. They are the leading cause of long-term or permanent disability, resulting in additional employer costs. These costs do not reflect the sacrifice of family members who miss extended periods of work, help financially, or permanently exit the workforce to care for the stroke survivor.

With advances in medicine and the treatments for strokes, the survival rate of strokes has greatly improved over the decades. Hospitalization time has decreased and the continuation of rehabilitation has become a home-based or outpatient activity. Strokes are devastating to the individual, family, and friends, both physically and financially. With rehabilitation, medical care, and family support, the average time to regain a portion of one's normal activity is about two years with vast majority never recovering fully or returning to the workforce.

In the late summer of my fifty-eighth year and just shy of my birthday, I became a stroke survivor...this is my story.

David Lawson
March 2018

The Seasons

IN THE MOUNTAINS OF SOUTHERN VIRGINIA, Mother Nature has her own ways of dealing with the seasons. The changing of the seasons can be a gradual, welcome transition with warm winds and temperatures erasing winter and easing into spring. Spring can be a glorious season of welcome warming with the leaves, flowers, and grass returning to their brilliance for the summer months. Summer is a glorious relief from the cold of winter; crops are planted, gentle rains and the warm sun nudge them from the fields, livestock graze lazily in the fields with their new young, kids play at the swimming hole in the creek…a vacation unto itself. Summer gives way to fall, as the winds turn cool, leaves fall from the trees, the crops are harvested from the fields, apples fall from trees, and pumpkins lie waiting in the fields. Fall is the time of completeness, everything ends and all are thankful for the bounty of the harvest and the goodness Mother Nature has shown. Fall then turns to winter for a time of reprieve. With the fields barren of crops, the cold and snow allow the fields to rest, to take in the nourishment of the snow and winter rains, and rejuvenate for the spring season ahead.

Mother Nature can also be cruel and unforgiving. Winter can be long - too long many would say – cold, with lots of snow. The snow arrives early and without warning, and continues to arrive leaving a thick white blanket on the ground that stays for months. It is then quickly followed by the arrival of summer, skipping spring completely, with scorching temperatures and uncertain weather that causes droughts, floods, and storms that destroy crops and property. The longer summer creates a shortened fall, one in which crops are left in the fields, apples are left unpicked and pumpkins rot. Winter is quick to bring its cold and snow once more, and nature's cycle begins again

On rare occasions, nature enters into an Indian Summer, a time where fall loops back to late summer, prolonging its goodness and enabling us to push the winter season farther into the future. The continued warmness of the Indian Summer is a welcome relief as it allows us to be more productive before the harshness of winter arrives. That extra time is a gift of Mother Nature, something of which we should be grateful.

Our lives follow the same pattern as the seasons, only we do not get a chance to start over. Our childhood is much like spring as we grow, planting the seeds of success and prosperity. The middle years are like summer, the most productive of our time. The later years are our fall season where we reap what we have sown…our time of completion. These fall years prepare us for our winter season; we get older and are not able to regenerate ourselves into something new. We look for the Indian Summer to keep us going, bypassing the late fall and early winter seasons.

Yes, Mother Nature, as well as our lives, can be very cruel or very kind, depending on her mood. Our seasons can change at a moment's notice without warning or forgiveness. An aspiring future created over the years with rewarding work in the seasons of goodness and grace can be erased in seconds with little or no warning. Our hopes and dreams, everything can simply vanish, never to be seen again. We are forced to endure the hard times while searching for the Indian Summer that will give us hope for the future.

And so my story begins.

Late Summer

AS A KID, I always enjoyed the summer months after school had let out that did not change much when I became a professor. Aside from my love of academics and the lifestyle that university life offered, the flexibility offered the chance to travel, catch up with friends, spend time with the kids and relax. With my campus classes ending the first week of May, moving into summer was a welcome and joyous rite of passage. With another successful year in the books, I was looking forward to the fall semester and most importantly, new plans for the future. The university had run afoul of the city and local citizens over housing issues, enrollment had dropped, and the administration had changed along with the arrival of a new strategy. Although they never truly explained the strategy, they say was in place and the implementation was progressing well. One of the thoughts was to move from an athletic model, where students were only there to play sports, to an academic model where education was stressed. The faculty, including myself, agreed with the premise but the students were in arms. Imagine being a student-athlete instead of an athletic-student, unheard of! But nonetheless, I had one more year left and I had made plans to move on.

I had penned an initial set of inquiry letters to other schools, mostly back East, as I wanted to return to the area of I called home. I had received positive responses, completed phone interviews with several and had on-campus visits scheduled after the New Year. I was at the top of my academic career, in my prime as they say, and ready to settle in and give a university many good years. Things were looking good for me professionally.

I had come back to the St. Louis area a few years prior in support of my kids. One was starting her professional teaching career and one was having career problems. I was needed and left a university outside of Charleston, SC to come back. The university had been a challenge but one which I enjoyed. They had decided to develop an online or digital education platform for the delivery of Masters level course, and signed a development deal with a major publisher. My role was to provide the academic oversight, design the class prospectus, select the content from the publisher, and review the finished course. A relatively easy way to build a course, but it was time-consuming and I spent a lot of time on campus. Little did I know they had hired a good friend and colleague from Virginia to design and build a residential program to directly compete with the digital program. They intended for the programs to compete with a winner take all approach with the losing program being deleted. I did not mind the competition as it did cause many problems, but I carried on. I endured the university in many ways but it was truly enjoyable in others. I worked from afar in southern Virginia, a major advantage, but I loved going down to Charleston. The environment was all one could want: the southern lifestyle in which I was raised, the charm, and the history. The charm, warmness of the people and the comfortable environment was something I missed and longed to enjoy.

My daughter had gotten a great job teaching second grade in a small school in southern Missouri. She fit in well with the other teachers and community, the administration and students appreciated the freshness she brought to the school. She was well on her way to tenure and had settled into her new home. My son was on his way to Pittsburgh, taking an executive position with the Department of Energy. Success was in his future. With the kids settled into their careers, I felt my work was done. I was ready to get back to a university in the East and finish my career. I would be able to bring the kids and grandkids out, travel with them and enjoy my time. I was looking forward to moving on. Without warning, my seasons changed.

THE FALL SEMESTER had been in session for about a week and things were going very well - as well as an Economics professor could hope. The students had gotten over the shock of actually having to come to class and create several workable economic models in spreadsheet form. It turned out that many of the students were "math averse". They did not appreciate nor understand the concept of math. A major challenge as a few dropped the course, but they came back as they had to pass the class in order to graduate. I had managed to snag a decent parking space in the parking lot and didn't have to walk forever, a welcome thought with the winter months looming in the not too distant future. The administration was playing nice as were most of the other faculty members. All was shaping up to be a great last year.

It had been a great summer, not too hot or too stormy, something the farmers appreciated and the crops had faired quite well. The corn was tall, the beans were high and the livestock was in good shape. The dairy farmers were quite happy as they could turn the cows into the fields for open grazing and water. They didn't have to bring in feed and water as in years past. It was refreshing to hear the farmers talk at the local diner of the good season and the promise of an early harvest. They had gotten their crops planted early and were looking forward to a bumper harvest. Mother Nature had been good this year. My summer had been spent helping the kids, helping my son and his family get ready for their move to Pittsburg, and getting down to see my daughter's performance in a several community theater productions. I was enjoying my last summer in St. Louis.

Throughout my life, my health had always been good. There were no major issues other than having my appendix removed, the standard glasses and a few broken fingers from my athletic days. During my time in Virginia five years prior, I had gotten fairly ill for the first time in years. No one was sure if it was a virus of sorts or reaction to a medicine, but I lost a significant amount of weight and felt terrible for quite a long time. I had trouble eating and the doctors wanted me to find something I could eat with regularity. Enter Hardee's Cinnamon-n-Raisin Biscuits. For some reason, I could eat them without a problem, regained some weight and began to feel better. It became a running joke between the doctor and me. She mentioned that she had not intended for me to ear the Cinnamon-n-Raisin biscuits, but sort of understood. They were the only things between further medical issues. She did stress that I would have to stop eating them at some point soon. Further testing indicated I was a diabetic. It was never clear whether the Cinnamon-n-Raisin biscuits were the cause or if it had been lurking undetected all along. Either way, the biscuits were out, healthier eating was in and I recovered over time.

It was the 27th of August, a hot and humid Saturday night, and things changed innocently but rapidly. Over the summer, sleep had become an issue for some reason. My guess was the uncertainty of the events at the university coupled with the anticipation of moving back East created a type of stress, not good or bad, but stress nonetheless. The only symptom was a constant headache which I had attributed to the migraine headaches I had years ago. Migraine headaches run in the family as well as hypertension. I had been diagnosed with borderline hypertension and had been taking a low dose of medication to combat hypertension. I had fallen asleep on the couch watching Netflix with a headache, gotten up later that night, and fell in the living room. My initial thought was that I stumbled on a pair of shoes or a blanket on the floor. I got some aspirin and laid back on the couch. Nothing serious, no cuts or broken bones, just a scraped elbow. Oddly, it seemed my headache had cleared, but I noticed problems on my right side with my arm and hand, along with a significant limp. Thoughts of injuring myself in the fall came to mind and I went back to sleep.

Sunday was a normal, sleepy day but the strangeness on my right side did not go away. With a new sense of shakiness, something I had never experienced, I could no longer hold a glass steadily in my right hand. I wobbled, painfully, when I walked. I noticed other problems when I ate and with getting dressed. The ability to walk became worse with each passing hour. But, I made it through the day and went to bed early - I had early classes on Monday morning. During the night I woke late again, got up and fell again, the same as had happened on Saturday. I thought the fall was due to my newly incurred bad leg and went to bed.

Driving the twenty miles to the university wasn't terrible, but the drive that Monday was not a normal commute. The sun was up, a great day weather-wise but traffic in town was terrible and getting to onto the campus was problematic. I had significant problems walking across the parking lot having to stop a few times to rest and regroup. Climbing the stairs to the second floor was slow, painful, and challenges with balance being an issue (alas, no building elevator). Another major problem came to light: I had trouble speaking. Anyone who knows me personally can attest that talking about something is not an issue, but I found I could not do it. My voice had become shaky, speech garbled and slurred, and uneven. I had lectured with a cold, sore throat and sinus issues over the years, but this was something new. This had never happened in thousands of lectures over my academic career. I made it through the day, made an appointment with a chiropractor to look at my leg and right side on Tuesday afternoon. I was sure everything would return to normal in the next couple of days.

As I left the university, the problems with balance and walking were becoming an issue. The distance from the building to the SUV was a level walk of a hundred yards or so, it was maddeningly difficult. I was having to stop and lean on parked cars to rest. Being embarrassed not being able to make the short walk, I had gotten my phone out pretending to answer a call or check for email. I skipped my normal stop at Barnes & Noble and went directly home. Having dinner that evening was difficult as the shakiness in my right hand affected the ability to hold a fork and eat.

Tuesday began much the same except there were increased problems with speaking and in walking. Another problem was noted, I had lost the ability to hold a pen and write. What I could write on the whiteboards was unreadable. Poor writing is a hallmark of professors, my scribbles could be deciphered, and I could usually read them with a second glance. But this was different. My daughter always said I could not write but this was at a level I

9

had never experienced. I could not raise my arm above my shoulder or hold the whiteboard marker in my hand. I made it through the day and went to the chiropractor.

As I hobbled into the chiropractor's office, I was unable to legibly fill out the paperwork or speak with a clear voice. The receptionist helped to finish filling out the paperwork which was embarrassing. The problems were adding up and becoming more prevalent by the hour. After a quick conversation with the doctor, he dispensed with the chiropractic review and advised me to go to the emergency room at the local hospital to get examined. It was the first time the word *stroke* was mentioned.

I drove the short distance to the local community hospital, tottered into the emergency room. After a quick conversation with the medical staff, I was ushered into an examination room and hooked to every machine possible. The nurses came by to draw blood and record vital signs and the emergency room doctor gave a quick examination. I was hurriedly taken to get x-rays, a CAT scan, and the standard battery of tests for heart problems - after all, I was the prime age for a heart attack. The x-rays and CAT scan came back negative, no blockages, internal bleeding, or other problems were noticed. However, the blood work was problematic. While none of the usual indicators of heart problems were present, it did show an out of control diabetic condition with extraordinarily high blood sugar counts. That alone could have been enough to cause major diabetic related ailments, but with the added symptoms of speech, leg and hand issues, their attention turned to elsewhere. Their initial diagnosis was that I did experience a stroke over the weekend. The high blood sugar count was not specified as the direct cause, but with my limited medical knowledge, it must have contributed in a mighty way.

My condition was well above their capabilities and arrangements were quickly made to be transferred to the regional hospital. My Fall had begun.

Fall

VISITING THE LOCAL EMERGENCY ROOM is nothing new as I have been many times with the kids when they were sick, hurt playing sports, or when family and friends were taken for a variety of reasons. However, this was the first time I had been for myself, quite a different experience. While nothing major was found in terms of internal bleeding or blockages (which was good), nothing good was happening either (which was bad). The fact I still could not walk, talk clearly or write, along with the high blood sugar readings were the deciding factors to transfer me to a regional hospital, one of the best in the area. They came in and told me I needed to call friends and family and make the necessary arrangements. What a shock! Living in a small town where no family close and only a very few friends, I did make the calls and hoped for the best.

I was concerned about my SUV and laptop as I made the call to some good friends to ask if they could drive it home. I also asked if they could bring my laptop to the hospital, I had papers to grade. I made arrangements to leave the keys with the emergency room staff and the laptop was safely locked in the SUV. For some reason, I was under the impression that a short hospital stay of a few of days was all that was needed and I would be back home by the weekend. I still had not called my kids to tell them what had happened, where I was at or where I was headed.

My friends made it to the emergency room as I was being loaded into the ambulance and I managed to spend a few minutes with them. I was trying to talk but I am not sure how much they understood or even what I said. The effects of the stroke were beginning to show and were getting worse. I was hoping for the best but somehow knew it was not a good thing. I do not remember any pain, no headaches or such, only that my foot and leg did not feel right and the problems with my arm and hand. From what I am told and understand, this is a bit unusual as there is usually a migraine headache to accompany the other symptoms.

I had never been in an ambulance before and it was quite an experience. As they were hooking me up to all the equipment, I was checking out everything. As a tech-savvy person, I was interested in all the stuff they crammed into an emergency room on wheels. They were doing all the same things as in the emergency room except it was at fifty-five miles per hour, a wondrous machine! The trek to the hospital, a thirty-minute ride through the back roads of farms, corn, beans, and cows, was uneventful. It would have been a great ride except I was the passenger. As a way to pass the travel time, I reviewed my Flipbook account via my phone as the ambulance had rolling wi-fi and charged my phone via a USB charging port. A truly wonderous machine! I did text the kids that Gene Wilder had passed away, they still have not let me forget that!

On the way to the hospital, I slowly began to realize that things would never be the same. They had changed and most likely not for the better. As Bob Dylan sang in the 60's, "...these times are a changin'..." Little did I know how much.

The Harvest

I CANNOT SAY ENOUGH ABOUT THE HOSPITAL to which I was transferred. I was a stroke victim, no way to pay for the care, no church to help out, and not a lot of close friends to help. But they were a Christian medical group and I was welcomed with open arms. Needless to say, after the doctors reviewed my charts and initial tests from the local hospital and the charts from the ambulance, they looked at me rather strangely. I often wondered if the doctors were asking themselves why I was still breathing; I know I was beginning to wonder. They kept asking if I was in any pain, specifically a headache, of which I was not, which brought a new set of strange looks.

The hospital ordered another round of the standard tests along with a few new tests to confirm the community hospital's findings. They all came back within normal ranges, which I think surprised the staff. There was no doubt that I had a stroke, a fairly intense one at that, but there were little telltale medical effects afterward. Other than significant problems with speech, walking and using my right arm and hand, I was actually doing fairly well. My blood pressure had returned to normal, my blood sugar had returned to normal, no blood clots could be found, no aneurysms or bleeding anywhere, nothing. They could not define what caused the stroke other than excessive stress and anxiety as a possibility.

After the initial round of tests and being taken to my room, a group of friends came by. I still had not called the kids, they wanted to and I initially declined the offer to allow them to call. For some reason, I was still hopeful that it would be a short few days stay and there was no reason to bother them with my hospitalization. I was anxiously waiting for a more definite diagnosis and further details, but in the back of my mind, I knew it would be a long-term stay. I was wanting, needing, it to be a short stay followed by a few days at home. All without them knowing and disrupting their lives. There was no need to worry them; they had enough things with which to deal. It was my problem and that was for me to handle. After talking with the doctors and staff, I finally relented and the kids were called. My son and his wife made the short trip from the city to the hospital. At that point, I was glad they were there - *I was beginning to feel bad*. My daughter, who lives about 150 miles away, had mostly fallen apart on hearing the news. She called, crying and concerned, and said she would be there as quickly as possible. She did come, sometime in the morning as best as I can remember. Both the kids were there, which was good, and I suppose they made the worst-case plans.

The kids called my friends to let them know of my situation and several abrupt surprises came to light. Other than two of my closest friends at my old church, a church I had attended for almost twenty-five years, they were silent; no email, phone call, no nothing. The pastor, who had become a trusted friend over the years, did not call as best as I remember or was told. He did come by a couple times over the course of the stay, but a very few times. I often wondered why others, who I thought were friends, did not call, email or visit. It became a burning question that I could not understand or answer. During my time at the church, I did my best to support everyone in their times of need, celebrate their good fortune, and be a friend in their times of need. I was not expecting them to visit in an official religious capacity, just being a caring friend was enough. As I thought about the developing situation it dawned on me; I did not have a friend on which I could truly depend. After twenty-five years of attending and helping the church grow, it was depressing and devastating. I have often been told that I am a better friend to people than they are to me but had never experienced it first-hand.

All of my very close colleagues from Virginia and South Carolina called, kept in touch, and did what they could. One of my dearest friends and colleague from the university came by within a couple days and kept in touch the entire time. I am very thankful for these friends; it is not until something such as this happens that one finds out who their true friends really are.

On Friends

The meaning of friendship has been a focus of thought. What is a friend? Is friendship an open and trusting relationship? Can you be a better friend to others than they are to you? Or, is there an underlying reason: do they want something in return?

Strangely the question brought quite a few surprising answers and revelations. Friends will come and go, but true friends will always remain. Although they will get upset with you, not understand you, possibly even discuss or say hateful things about you with others, they will always return your call, email or text, give you a call or shoot you an email, something to keep the friendship open. Friendship is about communications if one party stops, it is a sure sign of problems, most likely the friendship is in trouble.

As friendships evolve over the years, there is always give and take from both sides. Disagreements may occur, educated and enlightened discussion will follow and afterward, it is forgotten...hopefully. When the disagreements are held on as grudges and become the reasoning for not communicating, one must question the friendship. One attempts to cover with the ever tired "too busy," "didn't get your text or voicemail," or "you must have me confused with someone else" in direct conversation, Any attempt to be a friend is wasted time. You can't be a friend to one who does not want to have a friend, i.e. you can be a better friend to them than they are to you.

I have always tried to be a friend to all, never ruled anyone out because they did not belong to certain social groups or social status, have a certain level of wealth or standing, political or religious views, what they can get or do for you, and so forth. One does not select or maintain friendships based on criteria, one should be a friend to all.

Friendship is about truth, honesty, and respect for each other.

15

The summer has been a reawakening as several great friends have become "good acquaintances." The door is open to returning to the great friend status but it's their choice.

If going it alone is the future, then it is what I will do.

THE FIRST FEW NIGHTS WERE FILLED WITH THE REALIZATION THAT MY LIFE HAD CHANGED into a nightmare of uncertainty, doubt, and failure. It was if a ghost had come and would not leave. The guilty feelings of the past came rushing back. If I had been able to overcome the part-time status at the university, I would have had medical insurance, and possibly not be facing the medical and financial situation I was now in. Although strokes happen to everyone, the benefits from simple things, such as insurance, are invaluable in times of need.

Being unable to walk safely meant that I was confined to the bed, which was okay. I was wired with monitors and an IV that provided some type of fluid. I am not sure what was in the IV, but I suspect it was a better way to stay hydrated and an easier way to give injections. If that was the case, I am truly thankful. The bed had a soft electronic mat that could take a number of automated readings but was used mainly as an alarm if I had fallen out of bed, a wise precaution. But, the alarm was too sensitive and went off if I raised my legs, moved too much or adjusted the bed. Being the tech geek that I am, I watched the nurses when they came to reset the alarm and saw where the mat was connected to the alarm system. They unhooked it once to change the bedding, and being the good patient, I unhooked it after they left. They began to say how good a patient I was since the alarm never went off and I agreed, I was a good patient! It stayed unhooked for a few days until they changed the bedding again and found it unhooked. After the charge nurse quit laughing I got a stern lecture and the mat stayed connected.

After a few days, my vitals were still in acceptable ranges and the therapy group came by to discuss the regimen they had envisioned as part of the rehabilitation process. I was ecstatic as it meant I was getting somewhat better and thoughts of the quick stay reentered my mind. I was tired of being in bed, watching TV, and anxious to get moving again. As part of the preparations for therapy, they brought a wide, web-type belt to use during therapy; they called it a safety device. I was okay with the belt except they cinched it so tightly around my abdomen, which was already sore from multiple injections, that it was uncomfortable.

17

The first day consisted of learning to use a walker, something I did not want but was grateful for afterward. Standing was a major issue that had developed over the few days I was in the hospital. The effects of the stroke were becoming pronounced not only to me but the medical staff as well. I had walked into and around the room the first day, which was a good sign, but now I could not stand. The staff had assumed that since I could walk, hopefully, the stroke did not affect my coordination or equilibrium functions, but apparently, it had to a large degree. After steadying myself, the therapy staff marked a path out of the room and down the hall for the first walker adventure. They counted off about twenty of the two-foot-square tiles, about forty feet, making the round trip about eighty feet. That was the longest eighty-foot walk I had ever taken, and the most trying. Being unsteady and weak on the right side was one thing, but I could not make my body cooperate, my legs simply would not function. I shuffled along, very slowly but yet with determination to make the first forty feet - now I had to make it back. They said it was only about ten minutes or so, but it felt as if an hour had passed, and I was exhausted. The stroke had done more physical damage than I thought, but it was something I had to push through. I had to get better no matter how long it took. I was scheduled for more tests, different ones as best as I can remember. Thankfully the results were normal and there was nothing new was found.

The therapy staff and several of the nurses were kind enough to stop by and guide me through additional walker adventures, getting stronger each time and going a bit further. Until one day when an older lady passed me in the hall. I was feeling good about my progress until that day. As the youngest person on the stroke floor, there was no way she was going to beat me down the hall to the therapy room! I started to push the walker therapy, going longer and quicker each time. Strength was coming back, balance and coordination were slowly returning, and things were beginning to look forward once again. I became more comfortable with the walker and was able to navigate the halls fairly well. I do not know who the older lady was or how she is today, but I do thank her for the spark she provided. Without her passing me, I never would have pushed through with the walker therapy.

AFTER A FEW DAYS, THE CHAPLAIN CAME BY FOR THE FIRST OF HER MANY VISITS. It was a welcome relief to speak of someone of faith who could, hopefully, resurrect my spirit. Being a Baptist for the majority of my life, it was always stressed that other religious doctrines were "faulty" and the Baptist doctrine was the one true way. Foolishly, I accepted the myth that others were of a lesser faith and conviction, but the chaplain changed my mind. She was supportive and appreciative in that I was a person of faith and did not counsel me on the "correct way to believe" or try to correct my thoughts. She was solely interested in me as a person, a person of faith who had endured a life-changing event and how I was coping. Interestingly, my dear friend from the university was the same. His concern was for me and how I was handling the crisis. They both offered encouragement not to discard my faith, that the stroke could have happened to anyone, and keep believing that God was in control. God had bigger, better plans ahead and I needed to be patient.

The long-term was something of which I was not thinking, I was too worried about the present. I had often thought of giving up, however, after talking with the chaplain and my colleague, I began to put things into a different perspective. It was true that my career aspirations had come to an end, but there were other things that I could accomplish. What I do not and still do not know, but, something. Calls of encouragement from my colleagues and friends in Virginia and South Carolina offered the same; there was something that I could accomplish.

MY IMMEDIATE FAMILY HAS ALWAYS BEEN VERY GOOD ABOUT VISITING when someone was in the hospital, something that had been taught for generations. It's a southern thing about being nice and showing support. My sister and brother-in-law, Mother, and close cousin and husband, all came by the next day and on several days afterward. I am not sure they believed that I had survived the stroke at first and were concerned that I would be confined

19

to a rehabilitation home for a period of time, possibly permanently. I did mention that was not going to happen and I believe that surprised them further. I had always been labeled stubborn, hard to get along with, and a few other things I cannot mention, so it was not too much of a surprise to hear my saying such a thing. They too offered words of encouragement, thoughts, and prayers, and kept in touch almost every day via text, email, and phone, all of which still happen to this day.

The rest of the extended family, as I am told, called my Mother, but was strangely silent toward me. They never once called to check, talk with my kids or stopped by to visit. I was not expecting much from them, but I did expect them to continue the family tradition. There had been plenty of issues in the recent past and I had stated my disagreements and thoughts. Regardless, they went about their business and I was never spoken to again. My grandmother had an interesting way of shunning family members; she called it being "poofed" or "Put Out Of The Family". It was a variation of the Shaker or Mennonite treatment of being shunned and treated as unworthy. She had been known to do this type of thing as it kept the family in line. But she always let them back into the family as she made her views known. After her death, the "poofing" became permanent and one was no longer a family member in their eyes of some of the family.

After realizing that I had officially been "poofed", it did cause me a great deal of stress and disbelief. But I accepted that new status and moved on to get better. I often wondered what they would have done if I had passed, would they have come to the services? Provide any support for my Mom or sister? Exactly, what would they have done? Living in another state, a short hundred miles away, I safely thought, *"nothing, they would have done nothing."* Would they have felt sad? Possibly but doubtful. But that is the price of being "poofed." Then I thought of another way to think of the situation: Who was actually "poofed," me or them?

The second week was not so good.

The Turning

THE RECOVERY HAD GONE RATHER WELL during the first week, probably too well when given thought. The nurses, some of best around, had gotten me up and walking with the walker, which was a sight to see. But, I was mobile again to some extent and happy. Walking was quite a challenge, extremely slow and painful, but was hopeful the pain would diminish as things got better. I still could not speak well, very slurred and hard to understand, but I was doing the best I could. Movement of my arm and writing was just as bad and painful. Typing was painful and extremely slow, but at least one could read what I typed, albeit awkwardly and slowly.

Toward the end of the first week, they had decided to move me to the rehabilitation floor which to me signaled the end of the hospital stay was near. A day or so of speech therapy, arm and hand exercises, and some extensive leg and foot exercises and I was feeling fairly well. Then it happened, "The Incident" as they called it. No one knows exactly what happened, but I suspect that another stroke had occurred. After returning from therapy, I lost consciousness and fell in my room. Luckily there were no other injuries, just a few bumps, and bruises, but the concerns the medical staff thought had passed made their presence readily known. Walking, talking, right arm and hand use became more problematic and painful.

The doctors and my kids were called and I was quickly hustled off for more tests. Hopefully, a determination as to what exactly had happened would be the result. Another round of CAT scans, MRI's, complete set of blood work and more heart tests. Those all came back in the normal range and no bleeding or blockages were found. A test of the brain functions was ordered, something new, and that came back with normal functions. After all the tests, it was never mentioned exactly what had happened and I suspect that it is not known.

Afterwards, I was transferred back to the stroke and intermediate care floor and the process of care began again. A closer, more intense care was ordered, along with a review of medications. More tests fast became the normal routine. One of the additional tests was a vision review to check for changes after the incident. They had given a quick visual check when admitted and after the incident, I did notice a bit of a change. The incident had a minor effect on my vision that could be handled easily with my current pair of glasses. As long as I could enlarge the screen on my phone or iPad, all was well. The depth perception and long distance vision were still good, though reading had become a bit of a struggle. Looking back, the additional medical review was a good thing. I was pushing for a complete recovery and getting back to normal, but normal was not to be.

The abrupt setback, the worsening of physical problems and the realization that I would never get back to normal became was just too much. The early signs of depression began to develop. I wanted to go back to Virginia, the last place I was truly happy, and if the end came, at least I was home. Some of my dearest friends are there, it is from where my family originated and it was truly home. I have often thought of going back to Virginia but it is not going to happen.

The chaplain came by and we chatted several times over the next couple of days. She was very thoughtful, easy to talk with about my physical and emotional situation. She mentioned that it was quite normal for stroke victims to lose their sense of worth, become depressed and not realize one still has something to offer. Her help and prayer got me through the absolute worst time of the stroke.

My family and kids helped me through this horrible time. My son and daughter were there almost every day, talked with me about things and helped to restore faith in myself. For the first time, I was truly dependent on them for everything; I had to get back to some level of independence for them, my grandkids and for myself.

Three days into September....this was the turning point.

The Stubble in the Field

AT THE END OF THOSE THREE DAYS IN SEPTEMBER, things became clear…very clear. I would no longer be the person I once was; I was damaged, never to be the same. That realization was very hard to accept as I did not know how much use of my arm or the ability to speak or walk would return. For an adult and academic, these were the critical everyday activities and without them, I would not be able to function. There would be plenty of hard, painful and trying work ahead. I had a choice to make: either try to get some level of function back or give up. I chose to try, to relearn those things many take for granted, and to endure the frustrations, pain, and failure. I had to try for my kids and grandkids.

Walking and physical therapy were the most aggravating and painful. Learning to use a walker was probably the most humiliating experience ever, but a needed step in the process. Being a relatively young person, racing the older folk down the hallway is something that I am not proud of, but it was motivation to me. I decided that I was not going to be confined to a walker and I would do what it took to not use one.

The exercises were aggravating as I had lost all motion of my dominant side and I simply could not function. Lifting 2.5 pounds a few times was painful. I just could not do it. Learning to stand was, looking back now, one of the funniest things I could have done. I felt like a Weeble and would wobble, except I would fall down. I spent more time on my backside than standing, but it was something I had to relearn.

While the therapy was cause for aggravation and pain, it wasn't without its occasional humor. Being the youngest and a single male (fifty-

24

eight years of age) was obviously something they were not prepared for. The older ladies and I got along very well, laughed and joked about most anything, but they really got some laughs from the kitchen and laundry therapy exercises. The kitchen exercises were designed to reteach me how to get things out of the cabinets, freezer, and fridge. At this point in my stay, I believe there was a major concern that I would never be able to walk or use my right arm and hand very well, and all the exercises were done from a wheelchair.

The exercises were to retrieve beanie-babies from the cabinets and then place them back with a grabber. Yes, the amazing tool from late night TV and one can purchase from the "As Seen On TV" aisle at Wal-Mart. As they explained the purpose, being able to function in the kitchen, I remarked that I didn't need to put or retrieve things from overhead cabinets as I could set them on the counters as I currently do. The therapist looked at me rather funny and the ladies laughed. I explained that is how a single guy lives and besides, I couldn't use the grabber anyway. Needless to say, the kitchen therapy was not much of a success.

A few days later, they placed a basket of clothes in my lap was asked to fold them. I again asked why and they said everyone folded clothes. One of the ladies laughed and said, "He probably doesn't do that," to which I said that I did not. I described how I did laundry: wear them, wash them, dry them, put them in a basket and repeat. Everyone was laughing, including the therapist. The therapist then wanted me to iron some shirts and place them on a hanger. I said I did not do that either; that is why I use a dry cleaner, more laughter. Needless to say, the laundry therapy didn't work out well either.

Since being domesticated in the kitchen and laundry wasn't an option, the therapy sessions moved onto things of more value such as speaking, walking, and writing. These were sorely needed if I was ever to return to a professional life, or simply to get back to some level of normalcy. The therapist changed my routine and I gradually became somewhat functional again. I could walk, albeit slowly, with the help of a cane. They handed me a four-footed cane to learn to use while walking. Yes, it was the type on late night TV infomercials and found in WalMart's "As Seen On TV" aisle. I remarked that I may be old, but not that old, the ladies found that quite humorous and had a good laugh. I used the four-footed cane for the walking and stair therapy. It did help but I made a note to self, "by a nice cane when I get out of the hospital." I am sure I was the talk of the therapy room for weeks but I wasn't going to give up on getting back to some level of normalcy. Yes, I had a stroke and I had physical problems, but I was going to work through them as best as I could and find ways to handle the leftovers.

I could deal with a limp in my walk or minor problems writing. I could always learn to be left-handed, but I had to relearn how to speak. The vocal rehabilitation was probably the worst. Not only could I not speak clearly but apparently, I was mumbling with a Southern drawl, which to them was all wrong. I spent many hours reciting Me-Me-Me exercises and attempting to sing the Do-Re-Mi song with the therapists, all the while trying to get me to drop the Southern accent. The end result: I did finally get the capability to speak somewhat clearly for a couple hours a day, but the Southern accent just will not go away. It is hard to relearn a way of talking that one learned as a child although she tried her best.

Small victories did not seem like much but considering what I had been through, I would take them. I had to figure out how to continue building on the good things that were happening.

Recommit

Change is the only constant that everyone can believe will happen. For the majority, the change will come in small things that require minor adjustments. For others, change occurs as a result of a life-changing event, the death of a loved one, a medical situation, loss of a career and so forth. In the darkest hours of one's struggle, God's spiritual presence will make itself known - it is time to recommit.

Recommitting to one's spiritual beliefs brings one peace, self-forgiveness and to clearly see the path that lies ahead. Recommitting to one's spiritual side does not mean one has drifted or abandoned your beliefs, only that one is seeking a deeper and more meaningful relationship with God. One is seeking to understand your purpose, how one can impact others and use your gifts. Spiritual recommitment clears the obstacles that have clouded your view and opens one to new ideas, thoughts, and opportunities.

God has given one another chance to finish the work one has started, only in a different capacity - one can see clearly the road ahead.

Going Home

THE LAST COUPLE OF WEEKS IN THE HOSPITAL had been filled with boredom, aggravation, and moments of despair. It is hard to accurately describe the boredom of being forced to stay in a bed by sensors, wires and the inability to walk. For someone who led a fairly active life being confined to a bed was hard. Not being able to talk, take a simple walk, use the restroom or take a shower made it that much harder. It created questions the type of life could I lead. I could only think of being in one of those dreaded homes confined to a wheelchair, drooling on myself, and staring out a window for hours on end with no hope for the future. I was already doing that from a bed and had decided that was not going to happen. If life was not going to be at a decent level then there would be no life. Somehow, I would get back to Virginia, back to Appomattox, and the final days would come at a place of peace, forgiveness, beginnings, and ends.

Appomattox is a special place that most do not understand. It signifies the end of a way of life, forgiveness of the past, and the creation of a new beginning. For me, it was the peace it offered. It was the place where I could always find myself, reflect on the problems of my life and clarity would come. Appomattox was everything to me and I had lost that; I had lost my sanctuary. If the end was near, and I was convinced it was, I would at least be back in Virginia, back home in the last place I was truly happy. It was the only place where I could find myself, be myself and be at peace.

The chaplain at the hospital had offered the hope of something after the hospital stay. A part of me wanted to believe and I tried to believe, but being confined as I was a reality that was too much to bear. I was angry at myself and to be honest, at God more than anyone. I had come back to Illinois to help my kids get started in life and to do the work that I felt God had put before me. Both of those things were done and I was ready to begin the most productive era of my life's and *this* happens.

My dreams of a professorship, something for which I had worked long and hard, and returning to Virginia had ended. I was now someone to whom no university would touch or give a chance. It was not that I could not do the job, I just had severe limitations. I was damaged.

At the beginning of the third week, a group of doctors, therapist and medical staff stopped by to provide an update. Their overall thoughts were I was much better medically, hypertension and blood sugar were within normal ranges, there were no signs of clots or bleeding, and I was continuing to make progress. They were concerned about leftover issues with walking, speech, arm, and hand. They said that those might get better or worse over time, but they were permanent. They encouraged me to continue physical and speech therapy and to focus on getting better. The most heartbreaking statement to hear was I most likely would never return to work in a full-time position, I was disabled. Although I knew this, it was a reality now. The candle had been burning at both ends for too long and had burned out.

I studied myself in anticipation of going home. Looking in the mirror, I saw a horrible sight. It was not the reflection of my former self, but a frightening shell of my former self. Gone was the strong, healthy physical person with a joyous outlook of the future. I saw the new me, a person with obvious health and physical damage. A look of despair and uncertainty stared back. I had lost over forty pounds. Not a bad thing but not good either. I could no longer stand straight, the right side of my body was hung limp and mostly useless. As I dressed there were problems with the little things such as putting on my shoes and socks. Clothes no longer fit and hung from my body. Not only was I not feeling terribly well, but now I looked even worse. As a person who had always taken pride in looking one's best, the image looking back was depressing. I was thankful for making it through the stroke and working hard to return to some sort of physical condition that was well enough be discharged. But, I wished I had never seen myself in the mirror.

I was going home. Now what?

"Never Give In"

Sir Winston Churchill

Sir Winston Churchill spoke to the British citizens during the London Blitz at the start of World War II, encouraging them to stand firm and never, never give in. The speech was given during Britain's hour before the United States and many Allies came to their aid. This was the start of the greatest generation in the United States and Europe that has evolved and remained the past 70-years.

One has asked what that means to me, well quite a bit. I am Britain, damaged and alone. I have determined that I will not submit to the effects of the stroke. I will overcome some, how, some way. The doctors and other medical professionals, my family and friends, God and many others are my Allies. They have come to my aid and with their aid, I shall be victorious.

Ask your Allies for help when you need it. They will come through in the hard times and in the good times. They will help if one asks.

Be undefeatable, undeniable and a person of influence.

Never, never give in.

30

Winter

I MADE IT HOME ON A SUNNY WEDNESDAY AFTERNOON after with the help of my son. I cannot say how much relief that single event provided after being confined to a bed for over three weeks. Feeling the warmth of the sun and being able to take a breath of fresh air was priceless. One doesn't know how much the simple things are missed until one realizes how close one was to lose them. I was looking forward to seeing my granddaughters again. It had been over three weeks and I was sure they had grown quite a bit. I wasn't too concerned with the oldest one; she would remember me and be glad to see me. She knew I was sick and she understood. The youngest was just over a year old and I feared that she may have forgotten who I was. When I finally saw them, I got plenty of hugs and the youngest could not stop waving at me. After the hugs, they got their toys out and all was back to normal. My daughter had gone home and back to teaching, and I missed her so much. She was a big help the last week or so in the hospital and helped my son and his wife get the house back in order. Lord knows it took some doing but they got it clean. I can't say thanks enough.

After being home alone for a couple of days, one has time to think - sometimes think too much. I had gone from an active, independent person with a great academic and professional future unfolding, to someone who could not talk, write and could barely walk twenty feet without having to stop and rest. It starts a person to thinking, "can I *really* recover?"

What if I could not recover enough to go back to living a well-intended life or to take care of myself? I knew I was disabled but what if could not get the disability started? What was I going to do? My son was moving to Pittsburgh and going with him was out of the question. My daughter lives in a small town too far from the doctor and the medical support I needed, so she was out. I had such a feeling of hopelessness. Fear and depression soon came to roost.

Once those thoughts had taken root, anger made its presence felt once again. All my life I had managed to make it on my own, right or wrong. I had always made it and always recovered to a better state in life. I knew I could recover to a certain point but what was that point? I grew angry at the questions and the fear I let creep into my being. I was angry with myself, with God, with everyone. It was not totally my fault I had the stroke, but God allowed it to happen. With God's help, I could recover enough to carry on with my planned life, but that was not the case. The aggravations started piling up and I became angrier, much angrier.

BEING AT HOME WAS A WELCOME RELIEF from the hospital, but it brought a new set of problems and worries. Waiting was my couch, chair, bed, and shower, one never knows how much the simple things are missed. One of the most missed was the pitcher of iced tea in the fridge. One could say the I am addicted to tea and they are probably right, but being able to get a glass of tea without asking was great. At least I could drink tea and watch some quality TV and movies. Gone were the Oprah and Dr. Phil reruns (seen them all many times), the local news (which I never watched) and The Weather Channel. The Weather Channel was an interesting choice to include in the TV package. Being confined in the hospital and the bed, and not knowing if I would ever be able to enjoy the outside again, I really did not care about the weather. In their place were Fox News, the History Channel, Netflix, Hulu, and all my DVD's. At least I had something to watch.

As much as I needed and enjoyed being home, there were major questions that needed to be solved, both in the short-term and permanently. The immediate needs of how to continue therapy, how to get to medical appointments, and the weekly treks to the store, bank and such had to be addressed quickly. I was under strict doctor's orders not to drive and I did not know how I could manage those everyday tasks. Longer-term needs of getting disability started, continuing the medication and salvaging a career or starting another, loomed large and unanswered. With the determination to regain a level of normalcy that was yet to be determined, being mostly alone and without daily help, time became an issue as well. I could not rest and recover as needed and was pressed into creating new, innovative ways to accomplish many of the tasks.

Therapy had stopped at the time of discharge although there were several home health groups that stopped by to follow up. Once the medical checks were completed, they tried to sell services which I could not afford. Not their fault, as that, was what they were supposed to do, but it got aggravating to hear the sales pitch and get the sales letters in the mail. Looking back, the services were something I truly needed but simply could not afford. With no insurance, the kids unable to help financially, and no help from any local charities or disability groups, there was nothing I could do.

After enduring the aggravation of not being able to get the much-needed therapy, a certain famous speech came to mind. Winston Churchill, Prime Minister of Great Britain, made a speech to Britain during one the darkest of times, World War II. Separated from continental Europe which had been overtaken by the Germans, they were truly on their own. A country that was for centuries the greatest country in the world, was alone and faced the fear of a German invasion. Churchill rallied the British citizens to rely on their inner strengths and resolve, to "never yield to the apparently overwhelming might of the enemy," and that "we now find ourselves in a position where I say that we can be sure that we have only to persevere to conquer." The British resisted, help did come from the United States, and with the help of others defeated the Germans. The point is that when one has no one left on which they can rely, one must rely on ourselves.

The war I was fighting was between my mind and physical self. My mind said I could, but my body was saying no. There was no way I was going to give up at this point. I had fought through the stroke, made significant progress to get to the point I was at, and although there was no help in the present or the foreseeable future, somehow, I was going to continue forward. Remembering the hospital therapy, I continued with those exercises, often fighting through the pain and the tears when I could not do them but determined to find other things to help. I worked through simple exercises to help with the movement of my arm, hand, and leg. YouTube provided a welcome source of exercise videos for movement and flexibility. Although there are some that I could not and still cannot do, they did help.

Gradually, things became easier, allowing me to take short walks with the first of about a hundred feet – to the mailbox and back. A time consuming and exhausting event, but it was a small victory that gave me the confidence to take another walk, then another, then another. I was able to make it around the neighborhood, stop to pet the dogs and talk with the neighbors who offered me encouragement and best wishes. Although the walks were slow and painful, I came to understand that the neighbors were watching from afar. They would come out of their houses to say hello, walk their dogs or their watch their kids play in the yard. I just plodded along slowly and stopped to rest as needed, but I am thankful they were there.

Not having anyone to talk with for therapy was an interesting challenge and a humorous therapy to try to recreate. I got tired of the same types of exercises quickly and being true to Churchill's thoughts, looked for other ways to practice speech. Again, YouTube provided a mode of therapy most folks would find humorous, including my kids. While watching some videos, I came up with the idea to try to sing with them. They were a great source of speech exercise as the songs cover word formation, vocal cord exercising, range and tempo, control, everything I was doing in the hospital. As a classic rock fan, trying to sing along with Aerosmith, The Beatles, The Eagles, and the Rolling Stones was quite a challenge. Most would say it was hysterical. But it did work as I managed to create an intensive speech therapy that forced me to think about word formation, the sentence phrasing, pacing, the works. For the first week, most would not have understood my singing or the reasoning why, and with good reason - it was bad. I was never much of a singer but after the stroke, it was really bad. To my credit I must say, I did sound a lot like Bob Dylan most of the time (but that is a good thing…right?)

Learning to write was a major item to not give up on. My daughter says I never could write and it is true; my handwriting was horrible. I just never got the hang of it and it showed. Being right-handed and the stroke affecting my right-side, a new set of problems came to light. I could not hold a pen well and my arm had, and still has, a limited range of movement. I practiced and practiced numbers and the alphabet daily to try to recreate and relearn muscle memory and motion without much success. As much as I hate to admit, my granddaughter, who is now in kindergarten, wrote better. I tried writing left-handed, which was just as bad, but I did get somewhat better.

While in the hospital, I was required to grade papers for the university. I was able to use a keyboard and grade them electronically: I could type, albeit slowly. At first, it was the famous two finger hunt and peck method but eventually, I was able to regain enough coordination to use all the fingers with both hands. This was a great exercise as it provided a way to exercise my fingers and hands, force coordination, and mental focus. Over time, the typing got better and somewhat quicker. Although mistakes were very common, they were easily fixed with the backspace, and for grammar issues, Grammarly is a lifesaver.

One of the bigger after-effects of the stroke was the loss of focus. It does not mean that I am mentally impaired, I just could not focus. I had to retrain my brain to focus once again. Reading was a major source of both enjoyment and inspiration as well as a major function in academia. I found I could use reading to retrain my focus. Those who have read academic papers can attest that they are not the most readable, and in most some can be monotonous. On the other hand, books provided a great way to force focusing on a particular topic. I am blessed with having a good collection of books, most acquired while in Virginia, on subjects I enjoy. Rereading many for the second (or in some cases the third) time provided me a way to learn to focus for any length of time. At first, a page was a great success, then came two pages, three pages and onward. The process of reading significantly helped my ability to focus and as a by-product, the ability to focus my thoughts while I write improved as well.

Never giving in and finding ways to overcome the lack of formal physical and mental therapy helped immensely. I was able to continue making progress, often slowly, but progress none the less. I am reminded of the Marine mantra of "adapt and overcome." By not giving in or giving up, that is what I am doing. Semper Fi!

Disclaimer: I am not suggesting, advocating or encouraging the discontinuing of any prescribed therapy as the main source of rehabilitation. The therapists have been trained and their efforts provide wonderous results for those in need of their services.

These Times They Are a Changin'

Written and recorded in the early '60s by Bob Dylan, it represented the tumultuous times of Vietnam, the cultural scene, and the shift from a strict conservative to a liberal, more accepting environment. A trend that is still in place today.

For me, it signaled a new beginning of life. Everything I knew was now gone. My career had ended quicker than it began, road trips to my daughter's, playing in the park with the grandkids, golf (not that I was any good), everything.... gone. I could barely talk, my right hand was mostly useless for writing (and still is), couldn't walk...my physical being was damaged, never to be gotten again in the same sense as it had been. In a split second, times changed.

I have been told that the majority of stroke survivors never recover to the level they once were. I am one of the fortunate. I recovered to about 75% of my old self. With a cane, I can get places. Still can't write, learning to be a leftie. Can speak somewhat audible, for a couple hours a day. Still able to type but very, very slowly. Major issues with everyday things but I can get them done.... slowly.

Every day something changes, some for the good and some for the bad as no two days are the same. I have come to accept that change is a constant going forward. Each day is an opportunity and a blessing in one.

I am learning to live with the new me.

UNDERSTANDING THAT MY PHYSICAL SELF would always be in a state of flux with new challenges presenting themselves daily, never would I have imagined that such would be true at the university. I had been at the university for almost five years teaching courses, often on short notice, on an emergency basis or because they didn't have a qualified professor and being quite successful. I enjoyed the challenge and the students learned quite a bit as a result. I was well liked by the old administration but the new year brought a new, unfamiliar and unforgiving administration, who turned out to be unsure of themselves.

At the time of my admission to the hospital, I notified them of what had happened, canceled classes for a few days with the hope of continuing after an overnight stay, (little did I know that would not be the case.) After the new round of tests the next day, it became clear that the stay would not be quick overnight visit but a long event of unknown duration. By that time, the new department chair had called and wanted to know, not how I was, but when I was coming back. My son had made it over and called him back saying I had a stroke and it was not known how long I would be in the hospital. I did not hear the conversation but apparently, there were a few harsh words spoken at which time my son called the old chair, a trusted, dear and a great friend. I am told that a few calls were made and the tone from the university quickly changed. Accommodations were made for my classes as teaching assistants and others stepped up to fill in and I would grade the papers electronically. This type of understanding and accommodation is common at many universities/ At my previous university, I had covered classes for a professor for an extended period of time. But things settled down, the recovery continued, and the classes were covered.

The real problems started when I was discharged from the hospital, and sent home to recover. I was still under doctors care, and not released to return to work. The new chair kept calling demanding to know when I was coming back. Apparently, the doctor's note saying I was not able to return was not sufficient. The university process of accommodations would

38

continue. I would grade paper and answering student questions continued. It may not have been the most conducive of methods, but it was working quite well. His calls kept coming, my son kept repeating what was known, and then university human resources got involved.

Human Resources did not seem overly concerned that I had been in the hospital for three weeks, or that I had a stroke, and never really asked how I was doing or if the university could do anything as a whole - only when was I coming back. The banter went on for a few weeks and then I received an email stating that if I did not return I would be terminated. With the doctor's firm stance of not returning, my new limitations, and with the very common knowledge that most, if not all, of the buildings, were not truly ADA (American Disabilities Act) compliant, if I did come back, I could not get around. After a quick call to an attorney, the tone really changed. While I do not know for sure, I am under the impression the attorney called the university and spoke to someone. I am not sure how the university would explain firing someone who had been in the hospital for three weeks after having a stroke, had not been released by the doctor, as well as not having an ADA compliant campus; it would have been interesting to hear. At any rate, the new administration finally called with a more agreeable mindset. The new challenge was to get the doctor to sign off on my return.

The university had a list of conditions that I needed to meet in order to return, like lifting boxes of a certain weight and other non-job related items. In reality, they were setting up for my termination. The doctor had a list of conditions also: no stairs, no driving, and only work on a limited and part-time basis. Since I was considered part-time by the university, but on-campus all five days of the week and for most of the day, they were not agreeable to those conditions. But that was the only way I was coming back, on a part-time basis of two days per week and less than ten hours total, and all classes were to be moved to first-floor locations. The university was not thrilled about changing class locations and I am not sure why. It happens multiple times each semester, most often due to an athletic injury, and it was not a major issue to accommodate a student. The question in my mind was why could they not make the same accommodations? After several conversations with the new provost and doctor, I did come back for the time allowed by the doctor. All of this effort for what amounted to about a five-week time period from mid-October to the first week of December.

I never understood why the university did not do the right thing by simply saying to stay home, rest and recover, and honor my contract for the remainder of the semester. Discussing my return for the new semester could be done at a later time. A simple, effective and above all, the right way to approach a significant and sensitive issue.

During this fiasco, I realized that things had changed significantly. My career as a well-qualified and respected university professor had ended. I was no longer able to climb stairs, walk the campus, enjoy the often long days, and engage in committee work: the daily tasks of everyday academia. I did finally understand that things had changed, my way of life had changed, and everything was now different. The most hurtful was the understanding that I would never return home to Virginia or the East coast, a goal that kept me focused and moving forward. It was a terrible time as I lost respect for myself and became deeply depressed. I had to find other avenues to be productive and remain in good spirits.

IN MY EARLY 20'S, I was able to live in California and experience the craziness and the wonders of the state. Traveling around, I saw many interesting and unusual things that still have an impact on me to this day. I can remember driving down the Ventura Highway in a friend's convertible early one morning and watching the sun come up over the mountains or driving up Highway 1 along the beach. These were great times that I can still recall. One of the most impactful that can describe my life now is driving from Santa Barbara, down from the mountains, and seeing long, straight stretches of highway filled with stoplights. As the first light changed from green to red, the next did several seconds later, then the next, and the next until the all the stoplights were red, in one well-orchestrated rhythm. That changing from green to red is how my life is now. What was once an open stretch of highway with green lights ahead as far as one could imagine, is now filled with red lights that have stopped me at every opportunity, causing me to detour and live continually in a constant fog of uncertainty. Regardless of how hard I try, I cannot find the clarity of Highway 1 or the Ventura Highway.

While I have enjoyed many things in my life, there have been plenty that I have not and those have passed into distant memory. The saying of "stopping to smell the roses" is so true when one experiences a life-changing event and the ability to ever "smell the roses" again is in question. One is often asked if there was anything one would change in their lives and the traditional answer is no, however, I would beg to differ. There are many things I would change if I was able.

Being confined at home for an extended period is a challenge no one should be forced to endure. Thoughts, often horrible thoughts, come rushing back to what I had missed and what I would miss in the future. Those events drove me into a depression I could not shake. The stroke itself, the new limits of movement, and the lost career joined with the thoughts of what was and what never will be was too much to consider.

The depression most likely started in the hospital. The kids had made some observations and I did everything I could to work through the depression. The chaplain and several of the medical staff said that it was a natural event and with me being so young, fifty-eight years old at the time, it was a high probability. The depression really set in once I was at home. I all but lost my university job, was unable to do the things I once did and the future seemed bleak. I had lost interest in most everything I once enjoyed, the ever-present quest for academic excellence (which I learned no one achieves), and life in general. I wanted it to stop quietly and quickly. How it ended I did not care. It just needed to end.

Late night TV is a wonderful thing to behold. In my case, I had ninety-nine channels of not much to watch. Late one night I happened upon a special dedicated to those prominent individuals and entertainers who had recently passed, highlighting their accomplishments. I normally don't pay much attention to those types of shows, but they mentioned the anniversary of the death of one of my favorite entertainers, Warren Zevon of "Werewolf of London" and "Carmelita" fane. They were showing a video of another not so famous song, "Keep Me in Your Heart," that Zevon had written just before his death. The video was a visual showcase of the interactions in the recording studio of Zevon and countless entertainers who, in essence, were saying their goodbyes. Zevon had been battling mesothelioma, a lung cancer caused by exposure to asbestos, and was in the last stages. That song touched something in my being, helped to put things into perspective, and helped me to begin working past the depression.

I was so concerned about self, what I had lost and what I would never experience, that it was preventing me from the healing process, with much of it beings psychological. My mental and psychological state was affecting my physical state. Although I was doing the YouTube and physical rehabilitation, it was becoming less and less, and the lack of rehabilitation was beginning to be noticeable. I also understood that I needed to make those memories by "smelling the roses" with my loved ones so they would keep me in their hearts once I was gone. I began to send cards, email, and text more…I even tried to learn to Snapchat (still working on that!). The depression and thoughts of myself did not seem to matter much as I was working on creating memories that were much more important.

I looked up the last interview Mr. Zevon did with David Letterman on YouTube, and he said an interesting thing…if he had to do it over again he would "enjoy every sandwich." Apparently, he missed many parts of his life and wished he would have enjoyed his life more. Hearing that helped to begin lifting from the depression, to focus on getting better, to stop the self-indulging process of negative thoughts, and to begin enjoying life again.

Although I still battle depression, it is not as bad as it was then, and I can manage and get through. Tomorrow is another day.

"Enjoy Every Sandwich"

A comical phrase uttered by Warren Zevon on his last visit with David Letterman months before his passing. To many who didn't quite understand those poignant words, Zevon had been battling terminal cancer for several years. When one understands, truly understands, the things a person is going through, their thoughts and realities, only then can a person be understood.

Over the past couple of months, I have lost a good friend and contact with many others have dwindled. The missed chance for friendships to deepen and be a source of joyfulness for all have passed, most likely to never be available again. But that is okay, there will be others...greater, deeper and more meaningful.

While there are many things I would have done differently over the years, I tried to "enjoy every sandwich." There were plenty of good times along with periods of not so good. But in each season, the enjoyment of that sandwich provided the encouragement and desire to move forward. It is my hope that those moments provided a spark for my kids and others to never quit. I had jokingly made a short saying with my daughter when she was young —

AMP - Always make progress!

Little did I know how true that would be today.

"Enjoy every sandwich" means as much to friends, past and present, as it does personally. We are only given a short amount of time on Earth to enjoy life and others and to help some past their problems large and small. Maybe, just maybe, we will see our impact on this planet and others. We may never see our impact, but that does not stop one from enjoying the sandwich, being a friend to others and enjoying them every day.

When we stop enjoying the sandwich by ceasing friendship because of different beliefs, not running in the same social or religious circles,

political stances or different philosophies, one is limiting their impact.
One has to be a friend before any impact can be made.

I, on a quiet Saturday morning, will strive to be a friend to everyone
and "enjoy every sandwich."

THE FRAGILE FINANCIAL SITUATION I WAS FACING was bad enough and had a role in the depression while creating a time of urgency and uncertainty. Yet I was not terribly worried as I had a bit of money in the bank; believed I had the ability to find other avenues to earn money until the next fall when I would start a surely new position at another university. As long as I could continue at the university where I was, all would be good. The stroke changed the feeling of concern to one of panic. My good friends in the old administration understood and with their help, I would get paid until the end of the semester, but then what? The series of events that followed, that most would call it a comedy of errors, but there was no comedy.

My son filed my disability paperwork while I was in the hospital. He submitted all the documents from the hospital, the doctor, and financial statements. His past experience had taught him the right way to state the claim, how to structure the documents on submission. It seemed more like a formality than a major event. As someone who had been working, paying taxes and been a general, all-around good citizen, I looked upon the filing for disability and receiving benefits as something routine, that it was something earned, not an entitlement or a government gift.

After being home for a few days, Social Security sent a hefty envelope which my daughter and I thought was the information concerning the specifics of when my disability benefits would start and so forth. Wrong! I had been denied. With all the documentation stating very clearly the effects of the stroke, the permanent disabilities incurred and that I would never return to work on a permanent, full-time basis, I was infuriated. After a few phone calls, Social Security said I could get legal representation. This became the answer for everything dealing with the government, but with no guarantees. Like a good but aggravated citizen, I did as they suggested.

I called a few firms, many who did not want to represent me for various reasons. I did manage to speak with one firm entirely devoted to filing social security and disability paperwork, who directed me to an automated decision-making system. After filling out the numerous forms of the web-based questionnaire, I was informed to expect a response in a few days. After a few days, I received an email stating that the firm would not represent me. No particular reason was given, just no. I called, tried to speak with a human to explain or to clarify things on the claim, but to no avail.

Not sure exactly how to proceed, I asked around and got some surprising responses. The most surprising was that this firm only handled claims they felt would have a high percentage chance of being successful, and only represented the certain types of claimants. They did not represent the "professional", of which I been classified. They believed a "professional" would have long or short term disability programs or other types of assistance from which to draw in such cases. Normally, this is the case but with every assumption there are exceptions. I was the exception but no one took the time for an explanation.

Several friends advised me to give up, find some type of job I could manage and get on with my life. Absolutely the wrong statements to make to someone who could not work. A few more phone calls connected me with another firm, who after hearing my situation, agreed to represent me, a welcome relief. After engaging the firm, forwarding the medical paperwork and original claim, they said they would get back with me in a few days. The conversation with them was as unbelievable as being turned down by a computer. They relayed that my claim had become "locked" and could not be appealed or reviewed, and they could do nothing further. I asked if filing another claim would help. They said as my original claim was within a certain filing or review window and the system, Social Security, would not accept the claim. The only advice they could give was to wait until after the first of the year and refile.

The first of the year was only a few weeks away and I had the funds to make it till then, so I would file again on January 1. As a precaution, on I made a few more phone calls and found another attorney who could not understand the denial and agreed to represent me. He filed the necessary representation paperwork with Social Security and everyone waited as patiently as they could.

The university did not renew my contract for the upcoming semester, no surprise, and the financial concerns came to the forefront again. However, this was not a major concern as I was now unemployed without prejudice (legal term), meaning I was not fired. As this was a simple end of contract situation, I could and should be able to draw unemployment benefits without issue; wrong again, I was denied. The university did everything they could in order to not renew my contract and now they were fighting my unemployment claim. Asking the Department of Employment Security the reason for the denial (an oxymoron for a department name), they stated a little used educational provision that is seldom, if ever, used. It stated that a university could claim, without having to provide proof on their part, that they "might" use me in the future at some point. However, I could appeal which I did promptly.

After a few long weeks, a decision had been made. Denied again. They had made the same statement of "maybe at some point in the future", without proof or validation, and that was good enough for the state. However, the state made the same statement as Social Security did, and told me that I could get legal representation at their expense, and I did. As the new semester had started, it was clear that the university was not going to use me as the new semester became the future educational event. The paperwork was filed and a hearing with a labor judge was arranged. After about ten minutes of answering questions, a decision was reached and I was entitled to draw unemployment! I had succeeded in securing an earned benefit which helped to relieve some of the financial strain. I could make it a bit longer while waiting for Social Security to start. When that would be was not known, but hopes were high.

In early spring, my Social Security attorney called. They had approved my claim and I would be receiving benefits starting in mid-summer! A few days later, Social Security called and verified what my attorney relayed but there was a catch: I would have to serve a six-month waiting period and I would not receive any payment for the waiting period. After speaking with the attorney, he said I could appeal but that would hold any payments until the appeal was over and the final disability amount may be lowered. He advised against the appeal and I agreed.

Having had minimal income the second half of the last year and none for the first quarter of the new year, I was mostly broke. The victory with unemployment had provided a minimal way of life with everything going to pay the basics, (rent, utilities and such), with little left for food and medical costs. With unemployment benefits now exhausted and about four months before the disability benefits would start, how was I going to get by? I did the only thing I knew, I sold some personal belongings.

I had accumulated many things over a lifetime of good fortune, and I made the decision to part with some, including some dear, treasured items. Over an academic career, it is amazing the number of books one accumulates. Weeding through those was actually quite easy since my academic career had abruptly stopped. I can not say how many I sold online, to students or other individuals, but it was enough to make a difference. The rest I managed to get to a used bookstore, I sold those and was able to make it a bit longer.

Over the years I had always enjoyed playing, or should I say attempting to play, the guitar. I had acquired three guitars and a mandolin over the years. They were not the expensive type, but they were above average and of decent quality and tone. They played very well. I enjoyed playing them as they provided a way to reduce stress and relax. I would like to say I made the guitars look good but it is the other way around; they made me look good by sitting around the house. If I could sell those, I could make it until the disability benefits started. I got in touch with a friend, made an offer to sell them not for the price they were truly worth, but enough to solve the immediate financial problem. He tried them for a couple of weeks, bought them and I was good to go until disability started.

It was a sad day to see them go, but since I could not play any longer, I was pleased with them going to a good home where they would be used. I did keep one, my favorite, a 70's era red hollow-body, to use for therapy. It helps with hand, finger and arm movement on the right side. I still can not play well, but I have it. I will pass it down to the kids at some point.

Finally, the long, hard winter looked as if it was coming to an end. I had managed to gain a few victories, although small, they were victories nonetheless. Those victories enabled me to get through the some of the hardest time of my life. I refer to these months as "The Starving Time." The settlers at Jamestown referred to their first winter in Virginia with death, no help on the foreseeable future, and total failure looming, as their "starving time." Somehow they made it through, as did I. With spring coming soon, things would get better quickly.

Don't Accept Rejection

I am determined to reconnect with the greater society and become accepted based on who am I now. I never was great at dealing with rejection, however, now it is almost a daily occurrence. People will do various things that are not intended to be a rejection but end up being one. Having trouble speaking clearly for an extended period of time, they just will not talk with you. Imagine being in a group and have the entire group not say a word to you because you are hard to understand - the group has rejected you. At the same time, a very good friend and his wife understands the situation and is wonderful at listening to someone who has trouble enunciating words and completing sentences. They have accepted the new me and I am grateful.

Society has a terrible habit of only associating with whole people while throwing the damaged folks away - after all, we are a throwaway society. That is just not acceptable to me and I will not be rejected.

I have made it a point to seek out places where my damaged self is accepted. I will not be rejected, I will not be disgraced, and I will not be discouraged. Being continually rejected causes self-doubt and depression.

Each of us has a destiny that we must fulfill. In order to fulfill that destiny, we must reconnect with society and find those who will accept and help us move forward. I will reject the rejectors. I won't let others hold me down or back.

I will not accept rejection!

Spring

As QUICKLY AS WINTER CAME, spring came just as quick. As the grass greened and winds became warm, so did my spirits and outlook on life. I had made it through the toughest times I have known surviving the stroke, creating ad-hoc therapy, fighting the state and federal bureaucracies for earned payments, and loss of employment. Not to mention the frustrations, aches, pains and the leftovers a stroke leaves behind. Things were not much better but they were becoming stable. I was beginning to understand and accept my new life; I was learning to live with me. The hard work had planted the seeds to return to a new normal with new challenges. I could see a dim glimpse of something and moved toward that undetermined future.

Believe

As I was growing up I dreamed of what I would become. My first thought was to become a Highway Patrol officer, then the military but then things came to a halt. Things changed dramatically. My focus became how to manage and get by, not to excel or do the things I wanted or was meant to do, struggling for years to overcome something that should not be forced on anyone at any time.

As time went on things did change for the better and opportunities did become available. While a career in the military was not possible, I did help to develop and manage several major programs that changed how the military worked. I saw no combat but helped to save the lives of many of our fine service members. Something I was extremely proud to accomplish.

Things did get better as I was able to get the Ph.D. and began the most satisfying part of my life to date, being a professor. I truly enjoyed being able to work with brilliant minds of the future and help to shape their thoughts and embed the knowledge that they could become great at whatever they endeavored. I was satisfied and making great strides in academia. As everything never stays the same, the stroke happened and my academic career crashed quickly. No longer was I able to do the things I enjoyed.

As quickly as things change, new opportunities would appear; it takes a bit of readjustment to realize them. I could still be involved in academics as an author, speaker, and consultant, among other things.

One simply has to believe that one can still realize their dreams and be a not just a productive member of society but a significant contributor at a higher level.

As I STRUGGLED TO FIND NEW WAYS FOR THERAPY, I thought of golf. I was never a great golfer, but I was not bad either. One could say that I saw the course from every possible angle, which called for creativity on the many shots, but I always scored around par. The previous spring I had bought a new set of irons and a driver, using them a few times playing with a dear friend. Sadly, he passed unexpectedly just a month or so before the stroke and I had not played since.

On a warm spring day, I grabbed the pitching wedge and some soft practice balls, went to the backyard, with my cane nonetheless, and tried taking a few swings. It was embarrassing. I was embarrassed. Being right-handed and the stroke affecting my right side, all coordination and strength was gone. The club flew from my hands, which was nothing new as it had happened before playing in the rain, but this time it was different. Not only could I not grip the club, but the muscle movement and tempo were gone, I had lost my swing. I tried again and again for a few weeks, all the while it was becoming painfully obvious I would no longer be able to play another round. No worries, I could still get out, enjoy the weather and practice putting on the practice green, wrong. The greenskeeper was nice, even understanding, of my desire and need for therapy, but did not want me putting holes in the putting surface with my cane. I can understand his thought as we both got a chuckle from the conversation, but I had worked so hard for months to be able to walk and was desperately wanting golf as a continuation of my therapy. That was not going to be the case ever again. I sold my clubs.

The frustrations continued as I found that I could no longer hope for the same day physically twice in succession. Each day presented a new set of challenges; some days I had issues walking, various aches and pains that kept me up at night. Other days typing and writing was problematic and cause for concern. Yet others presented talking and focus issues, but I pressed onward. I was happy that each day was indeed a beautiful day.

THE MONTHLY VISITS TO THE DOCTOR had been good, no major issues were noted and they mostly centered around the aches and pains (the leftovers as I called them), and possible ways to reduce their effects. Issues with my feet were becoming problematic as they were in constant pain, nerve damage from the stroke and from being a diabetic. The doctor recommended compression socks as a help to improve blood flow and other benefits, to which I said I would look at them. Understanding the benefits of the compression socks, I did look at them but they are most likely the ugliest, most unfashionable socks known to man. I just could not bring myself to purchase a pair and decided to deal with the pain instead. Keeping my mantra of not giving up, I looked for other compression-type socks that were more fashionable and would provide the same benefit. As a result of the search, I happened to discover several different manufacturers, an athletic wear manufacturer and fashion designer. They produced compression-type socks that worked extremely well at a lesser price than the medical brand of socks. The switch to a compression sock worked wonders and the switch to a fashionable compression sock was even better.

As the leftover pain in my feet became manageable, I was able to make walking a larger part of therapy. I had mostly retired the walker and used the cane as the aide of choice. With the four-footed cane not being a viable option, I had mostly used the traditional shepherd-hook types of cane, very unfashionable. With spring now here and summer quickly coming, a more fashionable cane was needed. The shepherd's hook cane really did not work terribly well, it caused me to walk awkwardly and did not provide much support which I desperately needed, but I used it just the same. While walking through an antique store, I happened upon a black cane with a sterling silver grip, fashionable, but was it functional? After a quick tour of the store with the cane, it was indeed functional and quickly became a part of my life. A few weeks later while walking through another antique store with my sister, we happened upon another cane, an engraved dark brown with a brass grip, and it too became a part of my life. The new canes, or sticks as I call them, allowed me to look good, get around better and enabled me to continue with the much-needed therapy of walking.

With the ability to get around better, spring had indeed sprung physically. Spring is the time for renewal, as freshness fills the air. Gone are dull, cold and dreary days of winter. With the leftovers from the stroke being permanent, I was finding ways to overcome and create a new type of life, not cured but overcoming and adapting to a new beginning - I was making progress. The newfound ability to become mobile was not without its problems, not for me as I was enjoying the victory, but for others, their perceptions became a stumbling block to friendship.

Too often people attach the "victim" label after a life-changing event, as in stroke victim, cancer victim or hurricane victim. While they did suffer and are victims in one sense, more importantly, they are now *survivors* looking to begin again in another life. Their old life was in the past and they had no place to go but forward. As in my case, I did suffer a stroke but am fighting to regain as much of my physical being as possible. Along with the victim label comes the belief that one has become a lesser person of physical and mental capabilities, and are to be taken advantage of mentally. While the thought may be true in one sense, it is not true in reality. I am not a lesser person, just a different person and in many ways, a better person. While friends should be proud of the progress of being a victim to becoming a survivor, fighting to start a new productive life, they are not. Friendship should be based on respect and understanding between individuals, not based on social, wealth or political status. It is also not based on believing or following certain beliefs or views, this is where the problems began.

TENDING ORCHARDS IS A LABOR OF LOVE and a joyous way to enjoy the county way of life. Acres of apple, walnut, hickory, or pecan trees fill the rolling countryside with trees that awake from the winters nap to exploding in green buds that give a glimpse of what the fall harvest will bring. Bushels of fruit and nuts are gathered each fall, used in the making of pies and jams, or for snacking on a cold winter day. At the same time, the real work that makes the harvest possible begin as quickly as the last bushel is gathered is the pruning. Unproductive and dead limbs are pruned from the tree making the tree healthier, more productive, and the fruit more delicious. The process of pruning is an old process that is mentioned in the biblical parable in John 15, cutting off the unproductive limbs. The unproductive limbs can still be green from the nourishment given from the tree but produce no fruit. The nourishment given to the unproductive limb can be better used elsewhere to help productive limbs produce more fruit. Such is the case with an unproductive friendship. The friendship may look vibrant from the outside but is a drain mentally, physically and emotionally. Friendships take a vast amount of effort and other resources to maintain the hope of it producing in the future, or it may be a long-time friendship whose time has come for it to end. When the energy one expands on maintaining the friendship can better be used elsewhere, it is time to prune.

As the snow and ice melted and it became safer for me to be out, I began to again attend a small Bible study at a friend's home I had previously attended. I was able to drive a bit but night-driving was still problematic and something I did not do. The Bible study was a welcome relief to escape the confines of the house. I could share a meal, talk with friends and enjoy my time, but something was amiss. After a lifetime in church, I was beginning to hear things of which I wholeheartedly disagreed. The disagreements lead to fairly heated discussions that marked the beginning of problems and the eventual end of a friendship.

I had been shamed into attending church once again, to which I agreed on a limited basis. While I enjoyed seeing many friends once again, the majority treated me in a rather cool manner; they were nice but not as nice as they once were. They seemed concerned about my condition, but not *that* concerned. Knowing many of the congregation for over twenty years, I was shocked by the aloofness shown toward me. I once again felt as I did when I left the church four years prior, I was unappreciated and unwanted. I begin to understand that I was being showcased as being "cured" through certain individual prayers, and as a personal spiritual reclamation success. However, I was *not cured* nor in need of spiritual reclamation. While I appreciated the prayers as anyone would, I still could not walk, speak well, and had a host of other issues of which they were not aware. How could I be cured?

I continued with the Bible study for a while, enduring comments of being mentally impaired, unable to understand the teachings due to their high intellectual delivery, and several other "mentally impaired" insinuations during the coming months. After speaking with the doctor and loved ones about the comments, there was no mention or suggestion of mental issues. Confronting my friend, a critical mistake was made as they kept routinely saying, "You must have me mixed up with someone else." I quickly realized there would be no admission of saying such things nor a denial. It was a way to keep from being exposed and more importantly, an attempt to continue to belittle and demean me while trying to reinforce the "mental problem" insinuation.

I have often wondered what was worse: being lied to or being lied about. In this case, it was both. I am not sure why he chose to speak the mistruths or deny them when confronted, but the damage had been done. The issue caused stress and depression once again, something I vowed to rid from my life. The friendship came not to an end but was put into hibernation. It is my hope that at some point in the future there will be sincere understanding and then we can move on.

The visits from the chaplain and loved ones showed the importance of having an open view, to respect and value the other person, not a specific religious doctrine. Religion has always been an important and large part of my life. One should never position themselves through egotistical beliefs and attitudes as better, more knowledgeable or the holder of truths, and to use those as a means to gain followers. That is *not* friendship. Having friends and a church that embodied these things were not good for me spiritually, physically or mentally.

Confidence is a major contributor the recovery efforts of any survivor as they are starting over, facing uncertainties and seemingly insurmountable obstacles. As a stroke survivor, confidence is needed as one is relearning the basics of life. Those everyday essential functions are critical to redeveloping a quality life, one which a survivor knows will have continuing problems. As those problems are seen, they can be faced with the confidence that they can be managed, but often times the help of a friend is needed. Most often not for actual physical help, but for the psychological depth one needs to develop and to maintain strength in oneself. Strokes not only are devastating physically but from a psychological perspective, they are just as devastating.

Friends can play a huge role in redeveloping a positive mental approach to life, and religion is often a critical part of that redevelopment. While the friend seemed to be pleased with the major progress that I had made, it was apparent that he really was not. It was clear that he enjoyed being the superior physical and spiritual being. I had been lumped in with so many others who had survived life-changing events as mentally and spiritually deficient, labeled a lesser being in need of their constant guidance, which they are only too happy to provide. They were a friend, yes, but on on their terms.

The destructiveness I felt with this friendship in knowing I was not valued, appreciated nor understood, and my thoughts were not welcomed was too much. Those things were of major concern, but to know that I was being viewed, treated and referred to as a lesser being was devastating. It is sad to say the friendship fell apart, but the seed was planted in those late weeks of spring to break the oppression from the toxic relationships that had slipped into my life.

Enemies can become friends (or "frenemies" in modern thought), as long,
cold wars begin to thaw. At the same time, friends can become enemies as
they are unwilling to understand, accept and support someone who has
experienced a life-changing event. They are there as one gradually recovers,
witnesses the small but crucial wins along with the setbacks only to start
again. The setbacks become less frequent and they believe that one is, as I
have been told, "healed." They fail to understand that the events are life-
changing, never to be fully healed and one still needs the support and
friendship to move forward.

Often when a friendship ends, one gets into a "fight or flight" mentality that
that causes one to make serious, drastic mistakes that move the conflict to
new levels. It becomes as the civil war, a brother against brother conflict with
each side clinging to a belief. In my case, I was not hanging on to a belief
but the realities of the leftover problems of the stroke. I still, and always will
have physical issues but I have found ways to adapt and overcome as best I
can. What the other side sees is a return to normal or "being healed", and
they hold a disbelief in the permanent scars that one struggles with daily.

I have decided to not fight in order to for the other to see they are wrong;
they will never understand. I have also decided to not flee, change my
routine, move to another town or engage in flight in any manner. That will
only justify their thoughts, making their disbelief stronger, while causing
further problems.

Becoming disabled is challenging enough to accept and work through. The
hope is to get back to an acceptable state of normalcy and being, but the
scars live just below the surface of the physical shell, never to go away.

THOUGHTS OF THE FRIENDS THAT REMAINED WITH ME quickly overtook the loss of a long time friend. Being located in South Carolina and Virginia, it made their calls much more meaningful, thoughtful and encouraging. While they could not be here physically, they were understanding in knowing that physical progress would come, sometimes in quick spurts, followed by long periods of maintaining the status-quo. In the phone conversations, they were elated on the good days and understanding on the bad days. The email and texts were appreciated, although I did not mention how long it took to create a message or that I needed a stylus when communicating via the phone apps. They were happy with the progress being made and that things were moving in a positive direction. They are true friends for friend's sake; nothing was asked nor expected in return.

The leftovers were still present and often made their presence readily known. Each day was new as I could not count on yesterday as a building block for the next. Any progress that was made could simply be erased by the new dawn. Some days I simply hurt, just painful days to endure. I could get around to do things I enjoyed on a limited basis. Being able to drive over and eat breakfast at the local diner was (and still is) a joy. I had become a regular, was able to sit at the same table and had developed a friendship with the waitress over the years. My iced tea is brought to the table and my breakfast magically comes out a few minutes later, it is better than eating at home. Most importantly and to my surprise, the other regulars had noticed my absence and were concerned. I had been accepted by a small group of wonderful people, acquaintances that became friends. A rare happening in a small, tight-knit town. The same acceptance was shown at the local bookstore I frequent. They had noticed my long absence and upon my return asked what happened. Needless to say, they were shocked and concerned.

The loss of one friend had opened the door for friendship with so many others. The seeds that were planted in early spring were taking root. I was not the cold, hard-hearted person that many, including several family members, had labeled me, but someone who was appreciated and valued. The stress began to go away, I began to feel better mentally and I was valuing my life much more than in the past. There was hope for a new, better life in the months ahead.

All Things Must Pass

Picture the darkest of times, those moments when you are not sure what direction life will take you personally, your career, friends...most anything. Those are times of self-doubt, and bouts of depression take one to new lows never imagined and one doesn't know if one can make it or not. At those times, a job will pop-up (if only for a short time), someone will emerge from the shadows to be a friend when there are none, and it lifts us out of the funk giving us new thoughts and a new lease on being. Dark times affect all the same, often at the worst possible moment.

The summer and early fall was a very dark and trying time in the stroke saga. Through these times short-term, jobs popped up that provided just enough to go on, better days finally started showing up. The dark times were not as dark as they seemed...just overcast.

I was amazed at the friends who had been there year after year started to go by the wayside, too busy, too something. They no longer had time for a quick phone call or a meal. I will admit that the stroke did impact the long-term friendship as I depended on them a bit more for encouragement and moral support. I do owe several in other ways and will do right by them for their help in those darkest hours, for I would not have made it without them. But suddenly, they were no longer there, dropping me back into those dark times.

Through it all, I am okay, better and stronger. New friends are in the future, brighter days are ahead and a new future is waiting. Florence + The Machine sang that is "...it is always darkest before the dawn. That is true, darkness always gives way to light and the brighter days gives each of us a new hope.

I do wish those friends were still around to help me enjoy the future, but all things, including friends, must and do pass.

Summer

THE WORK OF MOTHER NATURE in the spring is an unrelenting task, but the results are nothing short of a miracle. The melting snows and warming days reveal all the pruning that had been done in the winter months. Trees have fallen, limbs have broken free from seemingly healthy trees, leaves cover the ground, and the last remnants of falls bounty became visible. The stubble from last years crops poke through the just turned soil like a broken picket fence. Yet, signs of rebirth are everywhere. New branches are sprouting and offering their promise, tender grass peeks through the fallen leaves, and seeds dormant from last year's planting are sprouting in the fields as it is now their time to produce this summer.

The summer brought a glimpse of the new life that lay ahead. Gone were many of the items that had produced enormous amounts of stress. Friendships had ended, some gone into hibernation waiting for a new time to grow. With many new friends being made, a higher clarity of thought was in place. The summer was a time of renewal and growth, the past was the past, never to be revisited again. Many of the things that were once important were distant memories. Gone were the overwhelming desires to move back to Virginia, becoming the tenured professor, or finding a significant other to help celebrate the successes I had envisioned. My life now was to be one of peace. Peace with myself, peace with God, peace with those around me and making a difference in society.

It was beginning to be clear that I had made it through the stroke. Many of the symptoms had passed, the headaches, the sleeplessness, the stresses and the constant worry. I had hoped the warmer weather would bring an end to the leftovers, but it only brought more of the same in different ways. Changes in the weather, storms, changing weather fronts, rain, always brought more pain. It was never clear where the pains would occur or when, but they always appeared. I could predict a change in the weather better than any weather forecaster; I had become a living, breathing weather station. The only problem was I could not tell you what would happen, but only that something was going to happen.

The summer marked the beginning of disability payments, something that I had fought long and hard for during the winter months. The beginning of the payments meant that I could carry on with life with some level of dignity and well-being. I was much different than most in my view on disability. I had worked for over forty years believing in the Protestant work ethic that hard work will pay off. I could retire on my own terms and live a good, productive final segment of my life. I had always believed that when the end comes, it comes and I was good with that. However, my end had come and I survived. Ten years ago I would have passed.

The battle with Social Security was not over an entitlement, but a benefit that I had earned over a highly productive career. While I was working to get disability started, they were, in turn, doing everything possible to deny the benefits and did for almost a year. It seemed as if they were wanting me to pass, which infuriated me. I had determined that I may pass but I was at least going to get one payment. Thankfully the payments started, I did not pass, and everything began to look better going forward. The availability of the disability payments meant that the summer would be a time to relax, regain and build toward the future. I was able to turn down work, something that in the past was not a luxury. A focus on recovery was now in place, something that was sorely needed. Summer had indeed started.

The clear skies of summer brought about clearer and focused thinking. Gone were the jumbled thought processes that had become stumbling blocks. The seeds that were planted during the talks with the chaplain continued to take root. The myopic view of what was good or bad, the centered thinking from a religious view were gone. The constant reminder that I was never good enough or that I truly belonged, another religious stigma, was gone. I could finally see these and many other things were not only causing severe stress but blocking the growth and happiness. A new day was dawning.

Over the years and just prior to the stroke, I had always been told that I was not liked or was unlikeable. It bothered me. I admit I have quirks that many do not understand, but I am not a bad person, just different. To openly say I was not liked was too much to bear, especially from close friends in the religious community. I had briefly read a short book titled *I Would Like You If You Were More Like Me* by John Ortberg, a pastor from the Chicago area I believe, that detailed a troubling but real problem in society and religious circles. I was not liked for who I was or my thoughts or beliefs. I was not like them, nor did I want to be like them. Not being liked meant little or no inclusion of groups, a small select of "good acquaintances", and a very lonely life. Over the years, I had several great friends who had taken the time to get to know me, understand me and accepted my faults. It was frustrating to try to understand why would others, especially from a religious group, would not accept me? I could never answer that question, nor could they. They could only repeat much the same: I was just not liked. Regardless, moving that to the farthest reaches of my mind cleared away many of the stumbling blocks that hindered my growth toward happiness and well-being.

I'd Like You if You Were More Like Me...

My...what a catchy hook and title for a book! Written by a pastor with the lesson for other pastors and leaders on how to build relationships with those in whom we can trust in the best of time but more importantly the worst of times. These relationships are built over a multitude of small interactions in which one strives to understand but also to be understood and showing the good and bad of ourselves be known.

Each of us strives to be understood for who we are, the best of we have to offer, those ugly traits we have, how we understand and see things, to be accepted and to use one of the buzz words, be transparent and open. It is then, and only then, can a truly deep relationship and friendship develop.

At a deeper level, the book is clear that one should not attempt to change a person into something one desires, as Austin Powers would put it, into a "mini-me." This may work for a short while but as people change and we lack an understanding of the change, the relationship deteriorates and ultimately fails.

We cannot expect everyone to be as we are, work long hours, put family aside, have the same beliefs or values, be agreeable, or believe that one would become just like me. Our attempts to create perfect people based on our own imperfect ideal, to "Stepfordize" them, will fail (watch the Mathew Broderick movie "Stepford Wives"). In order for a friendship to grow, prosper and become relevant, we must accept people for who they are, not how we wish them to be.

*Taken from a book of the same title by John Ortberg

TOWARD THE END OF SUMMER WAS THE ANNIVERSARY OF THE STROKE, if one can call it that. It also brought about another round of doctors visit. I had always dreaded going to the doctor as I was afraid of being told of a new ailment of some type, but mostly because I simply could not afford the visit. Being classified as "part-time" at the university meant no benefits, ie. no insurance. While I made enough to pay the bills, there was not enough to pay for adequate insurance or medical care. I had always felt that my time would come again, the one good academic position, that would provide the needed insurance and benefits. It would never come.

The first few visits to the doctor were quite expensive, but I somehow gathered the money. During one of the first visits, my financial situation was briefly talked about and through the doctor's goodness and thoughtfulness, I was enrolled in a reduced payment program. The reduced medical costs were a godsend. The visits were not only manageable from a financial standpoint but more importantly, I could see the doctor when I needed. The same was true for the prescriptions. The first few refills were horribly expensive, but my daughter enrolled me in a special discount program that dropped the prescription costs to a manageable cost. Through the ongoing efforts of the pharmacy, the cost continued to drop. Things were looking up.

The anniversary visit with the doctor marked a turning point with the stroke. The past year had been one of sacrifice, self-rehabilitation, loneliness, purging, and rebuilding. It also marked medical milestones that allowed me to push forward. The blood sugar and hypertension had fallen into normal ranges, the headaches were gone - all great things. But the leftovers remained. When taking everything into consideration, I was doing fairly well.

The doctor was pleased, encouraged me to continue with the good things and surprisingly, changed my visit schedule to every six months. I was shocked, pleased, and thankful. At the time of the stroke, I was in such terrible physical condition, more dead than alive. I firmly believe I was not expected to pull through, I had reached the end of my mortal days. At the end of the visit, the doctor mentioned that I had recovered to around 75% of my former self and that the leftovers from the stroke would most likely never go away. Some days would be good while others would be bad, and some of the leftovers would get worse while others may get somewhat better; I should have another ten to fifteen years ahead. On the way home, I was quite happy that I had made it against all odds, and had a decent outlook for the future. I was damaged, but I was a *survivor*.

The doctor's visit marked the end of summer. The past year had brought drastic change and reorder to my life. But the end of summer brought the new season...the Indian Summer. That time of prolonged goodness, of growth and productivity, and belonging. The question of how I would spend my Indian Summer came forward.

Indian Summer

THE PAST YEAR HAD BEEN A PSYCHOLOGICAL AND PHYSICAL BATTLE with myself to get past the effects of the stroke as best as I could and start life once again. Adding to the battle was the loss of my career and the battles over disability. A zero-sum event as the loss of one was offset by the gain of the other. No longer was I at the mercy of the university and the whims of the administration. I now had a less, but consistent, source of income on which to build my future. The question that presented itself was what to become? I could not go back to lecturing at the university level, working forty plus hours per week or back to government consulting. What could or should I do with the physical limitations with which I had to deal?

Although the doctor had mentioned another ten years or so of good life, that is not a terribly long time. Going from the prime of your life and an unlimited future to one of a few short years, the realigning of time to complete the undone things is important. It is as if I closed my eyes for a brief moment and when I opened them, the future was gone. The struggle for a life of significance had begun. One in which everyone would say "he was not a bad person" or "he made an impact."

The physical difficulties continued with good days that stretched throughout the week, followed without warning, by stretches of hurtful and frustrating days. My leg and foot would hurt badly enough to interrupt sleep or hinder my ability to walk. My speech would be difficult and troublesome, disappearing at the most inopportune time. The ability to write would leave for days. I struggled to find ways to work with the leftovers, often without success, causing frustration and stress. I realized that the leftovers were the reasons why I could no longer function in a professional environment, and they created social issues. The leftover physical issues caused psychological stress and pain that had to be worked through on a daily basis.

Recovery from the stroke is as much a psychological issue as it is a physical issue. Being able to accept the leftovers, their impact on the new physical you and your life is a hard but major step rebuilding process. I simply was not as I was once was, would never be, and only had the future to consider. I had never forgiven myself for having the stroke, continually blaming myself for the shoddy medical care I sought and the equally shoddy physical being I had become. The leftovers were not going away, they had become a permanent feature of my new self and I accepted the new reality. Accepting fate is the first step in forgiveness, the past was the past. I could only get better if I forgave myself. That simple step brought much needed psychological and mental relief.

One of the many things that weighed in my thought, creating stress no less, is how my kids would remember me. As a person who experienced both extremely good and horrifyingly bad times, I strongly believed the remembrance of the bad times would win out. A troublesome and depressing thought. How can anyone see the good one has done if all they can remember is all the bad that happened in one's life? My true friends will remember me as a loyal and kind person. A decent human being and family person. Someone who was always there for the kids. While the "good acquaintances" will label me as a failure as I made no difference in their lives (or so they believe), they are unable to recognize the small but significant things over the years that impacted their lives and family, and the community.

At this point, I cannot change the thoughts of the "good acquaintances" nor will I try. Being raised with a religious background, the parable and children's song of building houses on sand and the rock stands out. Houses built on the rock stand the tests of time, while those built on sand are washed away at the first signs of trouble. The friendship of the "good acquaintances" was built on sand. A hardship had been encountered. One of which they could not understand, and they ended the friendship. The fog that the few "good acquaintances" created resulted in stress and uncertainty and was something that needed to be quickly cleared. This was a major step in the psychological progress of moving forward.

The Future Harvest

ON OCCASION, CROPS FAIL IN THE FIELDS FOR NO HUMAN REASON. They can be damaged by Mother Nature through weather events, the soil can become overused, depleted of the life-giving nutrients or any number of other reasons. The fields have the deep, dark color farmers love, but the richness is missing. While the soil will try to produce, using every last bit of energy, its soul is gone. Farmers plow over crops; they are not worth the time or money to save. Plowing them over allows the failed crops to become worthy again. As they decompose, they enrich the soil with the captured nutrients from their leaves, stalks, and roots. While the crops may not have prospered as intended, creating value at harvest, they create greater value by replenishing the soil. Making it relevant again in ways the farmer cannot envision. Everything has a purpose, a time, a place.

The process of preparing for the last segment of one's life is depressing; life had caught up with me. The physical suffering, emotional distress, and financial issues of the past year had taken me to the lowest point of human existence possible. Yet, I battled through to create the lowest level of life I could endure. Many would call this a major boost to one's confidence, but not really when considering the other option of death. In many ways, death would have been a welcome relief to the many issues of the past year and in life. I would no longer have to fight the battles to simply exist and to start over once again. More importantly, the kids would no longer have to be concerned. However, I had made it through the year with the outlook of another ten years of life going forward. The task was to create, in myself, the person I needed or was intended to be. Someone that others could count on, one of integrity and trust. Someone who was confident in themselves, who understood that they were enough, and not reliant on the thoughts and ideas of others. What thoughts would guide me in the creation of the new me?

THE FIRST FIFTY-EIGHT YEARS OF LIFE could best be summarized as years of constant striving. The transforming expectations presented by society and family were always just out of reach. I was trying to achieve what others had achieved, just to obtain the label of "having made it." I desperately wanted to fit into society, something for which I strived growing up, but, never achieved. With parents that were not truly accepted or viewed as the same as everyone else, their perceived shortcomings were carried over and applied to me. The lack of acceptance created an open hole in my life and created a confidence gap that I could never overcome. Attempting to be accepted, chances were taken. When trying times or failure came, others were quick to point out that I was not the same as they were and would never be accepted. The chasing of career and family expectations was equaling damning, never coming close. I managed to get the kids through college, but, was considered a failure by some otherwise. The "close acquaintances" continued with their confidence-killing efforts, resulting in near complete destruction.

The stroke upended everything for which I had worked, causing me to re-evaluate the plans I had in place. In some cases, I scrambled to not fall significantly behind, knowing the future would be better. Thoughts of getting one's life in order became the focus. There were many things I had planned, but I realized those plans would never come to pass. At first the plans were many and varied, but after more thought, they were reduced to a manageable few. The plans could be completed over time and with a practiced diligence would produce dramatic results over the short and long term.

The guiding thought that kept circling in my mind was that I needed to set as many aspects of my life in order as possible. "In order" meant clearing the clutter that had crept into my life, clutter that was keeping me from realizing the whole life I was creating. It is often said that one needs to put their lives in order before telling someone else how to clean their life. I have no desire to tell someone how to live their life, but I wish for them to see my life and be encouraged. There were many small things that could be done quickly and could make a significant difference in how one sees my life. The immediate thought was to stop doing what I knew was inconsistent with my being and aspirations to live a whole life.

One's judgment and intuition provide the basis for self-improvement. I am a strong believer that each of us has an internal moral compass that tells us what is right or wrong. It guides the way we think, speak, and act. We do not have to abide by an arbitrary code of behaviors or rules that dictates our every action but instead should trust our intuition, the things we know to be true, and our culture. With my remaining life being compressed into a ten-year window, I do not have time to figure out everyone's idiosyncrasies. I do not want my remaining time to be one of frustration, but one of peace with myself and with the world. Unraveling my past means to understand the wrongs and not repeat them. This step is critical in developing my future.

STANDING UP STRAIGHT WITH CONFIDENCE, CLEAR THOUGHT AND A CLEAR MIND WAS TO BE THE STARTING POINT of the rebuilding process. It was something that started while I was in the hospital, but I often struggled with it over the past year. All the "failures" of my life where constantly reemerging, clouding my thoughts and preventing me from moving forward. The thoughts of what might have been were too much to bear. The chaplain and loved ones indirectly mentioned that being right with my Creator was critical to long-term mental clarity and help in the recovery process.

The past year had been filled with the exhausting effort on getting better physically, fighting for the earned and rightful benefits, and learning to live with the new me. Thoughts of clearing the past and making peace with my Creator was always a thought, but, not pursued in earnest. As someone who had been brought up in a religious environment, most of the family would not understand those thoughts. I did blame God for allowing the stroke to happen, for the loss of a career, and for allowing me to be in the position I now faced.

I made peace with God as a step in the rebuilding process. No longer would I allow others to blame me for their failures; a huge weight was lifted. No longer was I burdened by the guilt of situations beyond my control. Along with this release of shame came being forgiven for the past. My past has been filled with shame that has caused pain and suffering over the years, for me and my family. A new person emerged as a result of making peace with God, clearer thought resulted. I was no longer burdened by the thoughts of others or trying to meet their expectations. I was finally free of the guilt of the past. I only had God's vision for the future and moved quickly to fulfill the promises of God in the last years of my life.

Just after the doctor's appointment at the end of summer, I received an invitation to take part in an exclusive, as they called it, management and leadership coaching certification program. A few years ago, I had managed to land a part-time position at an online university and had tried to convert that into a full-time role without success. I often thought of leaving this position, but never did for some reason. The university had not shown much respect or support toward me over the years, but now I was being asked if I wanted to take part in a certification program. I accepted the opportunity, enrolled, and patiently waited for the program to start. I had never been associated with any private organization or academic group who openly asked if I was interested in any professional development. There had always been a catch, an indentured servanthood clause. I owed them something in return.

I was interested to see if the theories that I had learned during my MBA and Ph.D. programs were still valid or been replaced with newer thought. I had built a successful career in defense consulting, helping to develop and revitalize the business of war, all the while coaching military and public leaders on the importance of leadership. The consulting era crashed just prior to 9/11 and I moved into academics, becoming a respected professor. While the stroke has destroyed my academic career, the many thoughts on business and people remained. Were they still relevant or are in need of further development? Was *I* still relevant?

The certification program consisted of three classes, with the first two coming in quick succession. Surprisingly, the content was entirely based on thoughts developed in the late 1980's. They were the same principles taught in the MBA and Ph.D. programs. The principles I was teaching and coaching leaders on were still relevant. After years of being demeaned, of opportunities lost, watching people and organizations fail, the realization came that I was not a failure. For years people had wanted me to become like them, but when I could not, or more accurately would not, I was labeled a failure. I was doomed to be on the outside looking in through the window. Years later, at a time I needed a major confidence boost, I received one from the place least expected - a university who had never shown any confidence or respect toward me professionally. How ironic! I was still relevant! what boost in confidence!

I was not clear where else to search for thoughts on how to build a life free from stress and condemnation, the new whole life person. What to exclude was clear, but, what to include was not. Being an academic, I immediately immersed myself in research with the reading of books and articles. With thousands of books and articles on how to create a quality life available, ironically, they are mostly devoted to the millennial or earlier generations. They are very trendy and provide little in the way of whole life building thought. Sadly, they are not terribly accurate or worthwhile. I had done all the things mentioned many times in my life, been successful, experienced setbacks, persevered, and recovered. But none mentioned what to do in the latter stages of life.

On the other end of the spectrum are the works dominated by the thoughts of Tony Robbins, Oprah, Brene' Brown, Joel Osteen and others. Their approaches are more on how to embrace the person you are, become happy and finally, live the life you were intended - a whole life approach. Their thoughts provided the needed inspiration of what I needed to build the final stages life. In most religious circles, their works are not given serious consideration. In all cases, their works are based on Biblical and religious thoughts (Joel Osteen is a Pastor) but are labeled as misguided, self-seeking, or unfounded.

I pressed onward, reading a number of their works and finding their thoughts on a quality, whole life to be more accurate, more fulfilling, more sustainable. Many of the chaplain's thoughts and loved ones were present. They seemed to be much happier, more fulfilled, more *everything* while remaining a Christian. Why could not I achieve the same level of happiness? How can I achieve a quality, whole life when everything I read in the Bible or hear in a sermon, reminds me that I am a sinner, fallen short of expectations or the requirements to reach heaven? Was I not worthy, was I not enough? If I had been forgiven of sin, why would the Bible not tell me about how to be happy or fulfilled? Was being "saved" supposed to be enough or was there more? There was something missing.

In Dr. Brene' Brown's book, *Rising Strong*, she says, "If we are brave enough, often enough, we will fail." I had a moment of reckoning. The stroke was my reckoning, the ultimate failure that should have resulted in death. But somehow and for some reason, I had survived. At one's lowest point, having the confidence to get up and begin again, to achieve the quality life one deserves and to be that person of significance, is critical. Dr. Brown mentions vulnerability as a key to starting over and rising strong. Vulnerability is the ability to show up, having the confidence to be seen and heard, without the knowledge or fear of the outcome. For me, this was the turning point in the creating my new life. I had to rise strongly once again, much stronger than before. To be seen and heard for who I am, and striving to become a person of influence and significance. I had learned a painful lesson in the confidence rebuilding process: not to let what others think, say, or define who I am or who I will become.

TREATING YOURSELF WELL IS A MAJOR STEP IN MAINTAINING ONE'S CONFIDENCE level and outlook on life. To often, we do not follow the same advice we are quick to offer. We counsel others to seek the care of medical or legal professionals while we ignore our own advice when the same or worse problems occur in our lives. I am reminded of the story of a dog owner who goes to the vet, gets prescriptions for the dog and has them filled, and ensures the dog gets their medicine each day. They love their dog and want them to become whole again. However, the dog's human has a medicine cabinet full of prescriptions they refuse to take. We love others (in this case the dog), it is just we do not love ourselves enough to take our own medicine. How can one lead a whole life and help others when our own life is a shambles?

In treating oneself well, we should consider what is right for us. Not a want or something that will provide a short-term boost in happiness or ego, but what is truly good and right for us. As parents, we constantly struggle within our families to teach them to take care of themselves, become self-sufficient, healthy and whole. We teach our kids about being safe, eating the right foods, how to dress when it is cold, along with a host of other things. Along the way, we help others as we want to make them whole and vibrant.

Is it wrong to believe that we should treat ourselves any differently than we treat others?

As the past rushes back reminding me of all the times I did not take care of myself, the question of "what would my life look like it if I had" looms. The short answer is different, but the real answer is this: I don't know. Maybe better, maybe worse. Using the past as a guide, it definitely shows areas worthy of consideration. How I treat myself going forward will determine my path and help prevent one from becoming a frustrated, angry or cruel person. The confidence I fought hard to regain must be present. With that, the guiding principles of my thoughts and beliefs must be present and projected forth. People need to know who I am and what I believe to be true and valuable. In the past, I have not made those principles clearly known and it has allowed others to take advantage of certain situations.

We reward our kids as they do the "right thing" and one asks themselves "why cannot I reward myself?" The answer is quite simple. We are pressured by society and family not to reward ourselves. It is viewed as self-indulging, egotistical, or self-centered. As adults, we are just bigger versions of our kids. As the promises we make to ourselves come to pass, rewarding yourself provides the motivation to keep doing the things that are good for you.

Creating a vision and direction is vital to ones self-care. Too often we dismiss this and let the world take us where it may. Having a vision allows us to find ways to surpass what seems unsurpassable, to clear the obstacles in our path and help us to create opportunities. To do this we must strengthen ourselves, as Dr. Brown writes, "Rise Strong." Taking care of ourselves and redefining ourselves along the way. Standing strong on principles as they are what defines us and gives our lives meaning.

WHILE I WAS HOSPITALIZED IT WAS EASY TO SEE PROGRESS. One could compare the vital signs with those of yesterday and see a drastic improvement. As humans, there is a tendency to compare ourselves and family against others we have deemed to be perfect or someone who we would like to become. One must be careful on how one measures growth as one can fall victim to perfection. As an economics professor, I always warned students not to make a direct comparison of companies as no two companies are exactly the same. An apple is an apple, but an orange is not an apple. Ford is not BMW. Apple is not Microsoft. Coke is not Pepsi. Each has their own quirks, strengths, and idiosyncrasies. They may look the same at a glance, but they are worlds apart. The same holds true with humans; no two are the same. Many idolize entertainment personalities, sports figures, business magnates or other rich and famous individuals, and try to imitate their lives and personalities. Many do not understand that the person they try to emulate is a personality.

To get an accurate measurement of self and our growth, we only need to compare ourselves with yesterday. Have I made progress in a given area? Am I a better person today? Am I becoming who I need to be? We should turn our thoughts inside and ask ourselves the tough questions. We must accept the realizations that in many ways we are a better person and strive to address the shortcomings to become an even better person. It is from those reflective times that true growth and change can come. One must be honest with themselves in order to develop a whole life.

On campus, I was always amazed at the level of competition among the students, and sadly, professors. Their only goal in life was to be like someone else, be admitted to a club, or given an academic honor. Competition is great as it provides the motivation to learn and to push the preconceived limits one has of themselves. Many students feel the pressure of parents, the university, or athletic coach to succeed, missing the mark set by others, and in their eyes, fail. What the students do not understand is that they did *not* fail, they succeeded with their talents. They do not have to be perfect. It is a shame that others do not recognize this fact.

The same is true for professors. The pressure to be perfect is astounding from other professors and the administration. Professors are measured via the infamous evaluations written by the students as the university administration has pitted the students against the professor. The administration evaluates the professor against other professors outside the university in terms of publications and conference presentations, setting their version of perfection from faulty expectations. The pressure on being perfect is enormous and unsustainable. As a result, many great professors fail to get tenure or the recognition they richly deserve and ultimately lose their jobs.

In the past, I have fallen victim to the perfection trap. As an academic, I joined groups of which I had little interest, participated in committees and conferences which meant little in the way of advancement. All for the sole reason of presenting the perfect image to the administration in hopes of keeping the job I truly deserved. I was unable to pursue the things that mattered such as improving the academic quality of the course or research the relevant topics of which I was interested.

As a father, I can honestly say that I did believe that I had failed. The pressure that I placed myself under was enormous. I was not taking care of myself and not living a whole life. How could I help my family if I could not help myself? I would venture that over the years, the amount of pressure of not wanting to be a failure tied to a lack of confidence and superficial anxieties contributed to the stroke. Those pressures have since been relieved.

Looking forward into the last stages of life, I will not engage in activities that will induce the pressures I once felt. I will only engage in activities that are beneficial to me long term, such as working to get better.

There is a saying that once one is an academic, one is always an academic, and that is true. I can't seem to break away from the academic community although I am no longer an active part. I firmly believe that there is work that I need to complete and must do. There is no pressure, I can pursue as I need without the stress of being in fear of one's job.

Going forward, the progress I make will be measured against myself and not an arbitrary standard. A whole life is one of progress and personal fulfillment. As a survivor, I had to rid myself of the comparisons to others. I have realized that the person I have become is complete. I am enough.

"It's A Beautiful Morning"

Today I was able to get around in the convertible with the top down, not a major event, but something of which I was unsure I could ever do again. Feeling the sun and breeze brought good feelings and new memories for me.

Each day I strive to enjoy, regardless of what it brings. It may be sunny and hot, rainy and cold, or it may snow (I love snow, by the way), but a joyous day nonetheless. I will make each day the best day possible.

BEING GRATEFUL IS NOT SOMETHING FROM WHICH I SHY TO ACKNOWLEDGE. I can only be grateful for receiving medical care from the best doctors, nurses, and medical professionals in the region. They saw a person in dire need of care, worked tirelessly to provide it, and they will never know how grateful and thankful I am for their care. I should have died, but did not. I am now able to continue life, rebuilding each day and thankful for each day.

Gratitude is something that is missing with many of the people with whom I cross paths with each day. I hear the word "entitled" more times than not, and have learned to hate the word. I, as they, are privileged to have a short time on earth, the touching of many lives, and helping those along the way. I am grateful for the opportunity that life has offered.

I have had many conversations with the student-athletes who somehow believe they are athletic-students, and they are owed their degrees simply because they were athletes. Over the years, I have struggled with the entitlement attitudes of such students with little success. With an elitist attitude, they fail to acknowledge the gift of education that has been offered them. I have seen this attitude in the lives of many others, they are simply not grateful.

I have had the opportunity to talk with survivors of life-altering events, medical issues, deaths or a devastating loss. I was amazed by their lack of gratitude. Many were more attuned to the physical loss of their homes, the heart attack or surgery. They were concerned about self and what they had lost or could no longer accomplish. Each of us is to be grateful for the things we have, no matter how large or small, knowing that it could all end tomorrow.

There are countless stories of the last words of the dying. Many times, they speak of an unfulfilled life, which is hard to grasp given their status. They wish they had more time or to have helped more people. The question becomes, why did you not help? You had the resources, time and ability, tell me exactly why did you not help? It circles back to not being grateful for the things that we are entrusted with, and the wisdom to use them for the greater good. They have truly not lead a fulfilled life realizing too late, they have missed their chance to be a person of significance.

Having struggled with the fulfilled life question, I would like to believe that over the years I have had a fulfilling life, but did not acknowledge it in the proper manner. Too often, the listing of accomplishments is seen as egotistical and self-serving, and for many, that may be true. On the other hand, there is nothing wrong for recounting how fulfilled one feels for helping others. Those interactions, large or small, with the people we cross daily, create that fulfillment. I will strive to be one of gratitude, grace, and fulfillment.

The New Season

It has been just over a year since the stroke and a lot has changed. Medically, I would say I am much better, not cured, but better. I am still battling the leftovers and always will, but they are manageable. The stressors and their causes are mostly gone. There are a few, as there will always be in life, but I am confidently working through them. My new season in creating a whole life is a work in progress, ever-changing and more enjoyable than in the past. I am finally able to pursue projects that are important to me, adding value to society and those who surround me. I must admit that I truly miss academics and have thoughts of rejoining in some manner. However, that is a seed that has been planted and will take root at the right time.

Many will ask why I took the time and effort to compile these thoughts, as horrific as they may be. One cannot learn the lessons of life unless one reviews their life. It is quite easy to be reminded of the good times as they are always fresh in one's mind. As humans, we tend to bury the bad hoping they will never resurface. Oddly, the bad times are where the most relevant lessons of life reside. It has been said many times that life's challenges are truly life's opportunities. How we approach and frame the issue determines how one will react to the challenge. One can either push the problem aside and give up, or one can face the challenge with full confidence and the will to overcome. My struggles to battle through the stroke and recreate a new life are examples of what one is capable of doing. It was only through sheer determination, doggedness, and refusal to give up that I now have a chance to begin again. My Indian Summer has begun, a new crop has been planted and I will make the best of the second chance.

The feelings expressed in the book were real. The fear of uncertainty, loneliness, and depression are common in those who have suffered through life-changing events. Overcoming those fears is the first step in recovery.

Sadly, many family members, friends, churches, and society as whole fail to understand the fear and feelings of the survivor. People and organizations fail at an in-depth understanding of the person. I was fortunate to have the kids, a few family members, several great colleagues, and the chaplain to get me through the absolute worst year of life.

For those who may be reading this short book, whether you be a stroke survivor, cancer survivor or any other person who has suffered a life-changing event, do not give up. When circumstances beat you down, take charge and forge ahead. Be strong and rise strong! Few are given another opportunity and you owe it to yourself to take advantage of that opportunity.

"Sometimes the hardest part isn't letting go, but rather learning to start over."

Nicole Sobon

The following authors provided the inspiration to
Begin Life Again

Dr. Brene' Brown
Michael Hyatt
Joel Osteen
Jordan Peterson
Viktor Frankl
Bob Dylan
George Harrison
Winston Churchill
Tony Robbins
Oprah Winfrey
John Ortberg
Warren Zevon
The Bible

91352595R00054

Made in the USA
Columbia, SC
17 March 2018